本 书 编 委 会

主　　编：李洪涛

副 主 编：张利利　王秀东

编委会成员：李　斌　谢冬生　潘征新　毕建红　臧良震

支 持 单 位：商务部国际经贸关系司

中国农业科学院农业经济与发展研究所

内蒙古自治区农牧厅

辽宁省农业农村厅

吉林省农业农村厅

大图们倡议秘书处

大图们区域
农业合作示范案例

GOOD CASES OF AGRICULTURAL
COOPERATION IN THE
GREATER TUMEN REGION

农业农村部对外经济合作中心　编著

人民出版社

目　录

科技研发篇

贸易投资篇

Table of Contents

Research and Development

Trade and Investment

序　言

1992 年,在联合国开发计划署的支持下,覆盖中国、蒙古国、韩国和俄罗斯的大图们倡议(Greater Tumen Initiative, GTI)机制建立。自此,在各方的共同努力下,区域内相互信任不断加深,合作机制不断提升,合作领域由交通、旅游扩展至能源、环境、农业等领域,为东北亚地区的共同发展、相互开放和共同繁荣提供了良好的平台。

在农业领域,近年来大图们倡议成员方秉持合作发展、开放包容、互利共赢的理念,合作领域不断扩大、合作深度不断增强、合作模式不断创新,通过充分借助各成员方在资源、市场、技术、资本等方面的优势,逐步形成优势互补,农业合作呈现出新的局面。尤其是 2013 年中国"一带一路"倡议的提出,进一步深化了大图们倡议成员方在农业领域的共同发展,逐步构建起利益共同体和责任共同体,各成员方在资本、技术、人才、市场等方面的互通机制逐步建立,区域农业合作机制更趋稳定,多双边农业合作逐步走向共赢之路。

本书立足区域内已有农业合作项目,精心筛选了涵盖科技合作、贸易合作、投资合作、园区建设等领域的大图们区域农业合作示范案例,并对其进行介绍和分析,以期为区域内协同发展提供借鉴。

"潮平两岸阔,风正一帆悬。"大图们区域农业合作之舟必将在辽阔的图们江上驶向更加辉煌的未来。

2020 年 5 月

Preface

Thanks to the support of the United Nations Development Programme, the Greater Tumen Initiative(GTI) mechanism, covering P.R.China, Mongolia, the ROK, and Russia, was established in 1992. Since then, with the joint efforts of all parties, mutual trust and cooperation mechanisms in this region have been continuously improved, and the cooperation areas have been expanded from transportation and tourism to trade, energy, environment, agriculture, etc., which provides a good platform for common development, mutual opening up and common prosperity of Northeast Asia.

In agriculture, member stateshave adhered to the vision of cooperative development, openness and inclusiveness, and mutual benefit in recent years.And the areas, depth, and modes of cooperation continue to expand by making full use of the complementary advantages of member countries in resources, market, technology, capital, etc., breaking new ground in agricultural cooperation.In particular, the launch of China's "Belt and Road Initiative" in 2013 has further deepened the common development of member countries in agriculture, and gradually built a community of shared interests and responsibility. The exchange mechanisms of capital, technology, talent and market among member countries have been gradually established, the regional agricultural cooperation mechanism has become more stable, and the multilateral and bilateral agricultural cooperation has moved towards a win-win road.

Based on the existing agricultural cooperation projects in the region, this book selects some projects covering scientific and technological cooperation, trade and investment cooperation, economic zone construction etc..Introducing and analyzing these good practies of agicultural Cooperation in the Greates Tumen Region, in order to provide reperence for Coordinated development in the region.

As the old saying goes, "from shore to shore it is wide at high tide, and before fair wind a sail is lifting". The great ship of agricultural cooperation in the Greater Tumen Region(GTR) will surely sail towards brighter future along the Tumen River.

5/2020

绪　论

·◇·

大图们倡议是东北亚地区目前最为活跃的政府间合作机制之一，大图们区域范围主要包括中国吉林省全境、辽宁省的丹东市、黑龙江省的牡丹江市和内蒙古自治区兴安盟等部分区域，蒙古国东部省区，韩国部分港口城市，俄罗斯滨海边疆区的部分地区。借助于地域优势，大图们倡议成员方在农业领域不断深化合作，并取得了显著成效。以中国吉林省为例，截至2018年，吉林省在俄罗斯从事农业开发的企业达到30多家，其中在俄罗斯滨海边疆区从事农业开发的企业高达20多家，约占吉林省在俄农业企业的80%。

除了合作程度深入以外，近年来，大图们倡议成员方在具体的农业领域方面的合作也呈现多样化的趋势，如中国的辽宁省与俄罗斯推动的"中俄粮食走廊项目"、"中俄放心菜篮子中心项目"、远洋渔业开发和海产养殖等，大图们区域的不同地区充分发挥地缘优势，积极开展农业合作与开发，多双边在经济、社会、生态等方面均取得较好成效。

一、大图们区域农业合作的主要模式

大图们区域农业合作的主体主要包含政府部门、科研院所、企业等,由于合作目的不同,不同主体在农业合作过程中呈现出不同的合作模式,总体而言,当前大图们区域农业合作模式主要有三类。

(一)以科技研发为主导的农业合作模式

以农业的高科技研发为重点,以新品种的培育为导向,在种质资源开发、作物栽培育种技术、农作物良种等方面开展共同研发,极大地推动了农业科技进步,也为大图们区域农业的高质量发展奠定了坚实的基础。以科技为导向的农业合作模式的参与主体通常以科研院所为主,通过政府部门搭建产学研平台,将农业企业进一步融入农业合作研发中,进一步拓宽了农业合作的范围。

根据参与主体的不同,以农业科技研发为导向的农业合作模式可以分为两类。

第一类是以政府部门和农业科研院所为主体的农业科技合作开发模式。这类模式也是当前大图们区域开展农业科技合作的主要方式。例如,韩国政府与蒙古国政府签订农业合作协议,由蒙古国生命科学大学牵头开展适合蒙古国环境的农业科技合作,目前已经完成饲用作物(苜蓿)良种繁育试点项目,采用粗饲料和强化营养技术提高羔羊和羊毛的产量及遗传价值项目,农业科研、培训和生产示范农场项目等农业科技项目的合作,合作效果极为显著;中国吉林省白城市农业科学院与以俄罗斯国家科学院为首的多家俄罗斯农业科研机构开展农业科技合作,共建中俄特色农业国际联合实验室,推进两国特色农作物新品种选育、高效栽培技术集成、特色农产品加工利用等关键领域的技术突破与创新;中国内蒙古自治区农牧业科学院与俄罗斯建立了"内蒙古中俄植物技术研究合作中心",通过与俄罗斯瓦维洛夫植物遗传资源研究所、沃罗涅日国立大学等单位实施中俄科技合作项目,在甜菜、玉米、菊芋、小麦、汉麻等农作物育种栽培技术研究领域不断取得新的进展。

第二类是以农业科研院所和企业单位为主体的农业科技合作开发模式,即以农业科研院所为农业科技合作研发主体、企业为科研成果推广主体,不同单位协作推动农业科技由科学研究落实到具体实践。其中较为典型的案例是中国内蒙古自治区农牧业科学院农畜产品加工研究所与内蒙古自治区兴安盟科右中旗特牧牧业开发有限公司、蒙古国BORNUUR ECO FOODS 公司等共同合作开展"抗寒水稻、大豆种植试验推广基地建设项目",取得了较好的成果。

(二)以跨境投资为主导的农业合作模式

以农业项目跨境投资为导向的合作模式主要以农业企业为主体,通过在境外投资建设等方式,搭建境内外合作平台,借助不同区域的资源、市场、资金、人才、技术等优势,在农业产业链条上不断延伸,实现不同主体的协作发展。在具体实践中,呈现出三个特点。

一是跨境投资开发的涵盖范围较为广泛。例如,从当前的农业投资建设内容来看,2018 年以来开展的两届韩国—俄罗斯农业企业对话会上,共签订价值 24.6 万美元的两项作物加工设施采购合同,签署 11 项农业高科技合作的谅解备忘录,涉及领域涵盖智慧农场和无人机等。较早参与俄罗斯远东地区建设的中国辽宁省在俄罗斯远东地区投资涉及农业种植、农产品加工、果蔬仓储贸易、畜牧养殖业及渔业捕捞等多个具体领域;中国吉林省在俄罗斯滨海地区从事农业开发的 20 多家企业中,涉及的产业类别也很丰富,如吉林省金达海外农业开发投资有限公司、宇尧实业(上海)有限公司、延边卫峰国际贸易有限公司、珲春华瑞参业生物工程股份有限公司等企业在俄罗斯远东地区开展了大豆、人参、食用菌、苜蓿草等种植项目。

二是跨境投资开发主要借助于双方资源互补的优势,即投资方和被投资区域能够充分利用土地、劳动力、资本、市场等优势,降低投资方的生产成本,并同时为被投资区域的发展带来可观的经济效益和社会效益。例如,中国内蒙古自治区满洲里市德丰贸易有限责任公司在俄罗斯伊尔库茨克市投资 500 余万元建设跨境农产品分拨配送中心,项目的开展有效地推动了农产品跨境销售服务水平,增强了果菜在俄罗斯远东地区的市场竞争力和影响力,促进菜农果农增产增收;中国内蒙古自治区维信羊绒集团在蒙古国成立羊绒初级加工企业,企业生产成本得到降低。

三是跨境投资开发方向也由传统产业向新型产业转变,逐步实现产业转型升级,即以涉农企业作为牵头单位,以市场为导向,在传统种植业和养殖业的基础上,在境外开发农业综合项目,开展农产品生产、加工、进出口贸易等业务,参与农业产业链条的多个环节,实现农业产业的融合发展。2016 年中国吉林省吉蒙农牧产业发展有限公司在蒙古国苏赫巴特省图门曹克图县获得 2.5 万公顷农业用地土地使用权,建设用地 120 公顷,计划投资 1.2 亿美元建设"吉蒙生态农牧产业国际合作园",将实现农业产业的全方位对接,极大地促进当地农业经济的发展。

(三)以国际贸易为主导的农业合作模式

以市场需求为导向,通过以国际贸易为主导的农业合作模式,突出区域发展的鲜明特点和潜在优势,进而形成跨区域、跨产业的农业多功能发展,最终实现大图们区域农业的共同协作发展。在国际贸易方面,当前大图们区域的农业发展取得了显著成效。

总体来看,以国际贸易为主导的农业合作模式大致可以分为三类。

第一类是普通贸易模式,即商品生产地和集散地集中在境内,境内企业通过与外方建立的长期合作渠道和贸易伙伴关系开展农产品国际贸易,这类贸易模式也为当前较多企业所使用。如中国内蒙古自治区包头市北辰饲料科技有限责任公司与蒙古国乌兰巴托市 AJIGANA 有限责任公司、蒙古国乌兰巴托市 Tumen Shuvuut 有限责任公司开展农产品进出口贸易合作业务,为双方企业合作共赢作出了积极贡献,中国包头北辰饲料科技有限责任公司从 2010 年开始连续向蒙古国乌兰巴托市 AJIGANA 有限责任公司和蒙古国乌兰巴托市 Tumen Shuvuut 有限责任公司出口蛋鸡饲料,年均出口蛋鸡饲料 7000 吨,年均出口贸易额达 330 万美元,此外,公司从 2010 年开始从蒙古国进口麸皮,年均进口麸皮 4000 吨,年均进口贸易额为 80 万美元。

第二类是搭建境外贸易平台模式,即通过构建境外贸易平台,不断深化与外方的合作程度,进而拓展自身的业务范围。如中国内蒙古自治区满洲里市德丰贸易有限公司与俄罗斯开展果蔬贸易、仓储物流配送中心建设,目前已完成恒温保鲜库主体工程和果蔬加工分拨配送处理中心主体工程,通过项目建设,有效地提升了农产品跨境配送销售服务水平,进一步增强了该公司果蔬等农产品在俄罗斯远东地区的市场竞争力和影响力。

第三类是基于产业链协作分工的国际贸易模式,即涉农企业通过坚持走境内资源与境外市场相结合的发展道路,与境外企业签订长期合作协议,在产业链上实现协作分工,并在贸易过程中结合自身资源优势开展合作,进一步强化双方在农产品贸易合作过程中的稳定性,实现双方互惠互利。中国内蒙古自治区维信羊绒集团与蒙古国宏聚有限责任公司经过双方友好协商,2019 年达成收购 500—1000 吨洗净山羊绒的协议,项目总投资约 4.5 亿元人民币,到 2020 年年底完成,根据协议要求,中国内蒙古维信羊绒集团与蒙古国宏聚有限责任公司将分别展开工作,其中,蒙方负责洗净山羊绒的收购、加工、检验、检疫、运输、出口报关手续等,中方则负责筹集资金、验货接货等业务。

二、大图们区域农业合作参与主体的主要做法

大图们区域农业合作的参与主体具有多样化特征,因此不同主体的做法也有所不同。从宏观层面来看,政府部门是推动大图们区域农业合作的引路者,通过制定规划、创设政策等方式促进农业贸易、投资与科技等合作;从微观层面来看,科研单位和企业是推动大图们区域实现农业合作的中坚力量。

(一)搭建科学研究平台,科技助力区域合作

集合农业领域中科研、教育、生产等不同社会分工,综合其功能与优势,实现农业技术创新中不同环节的对接和耦合,进而推动大图们区域内农业技术的共同发展。从当前大图们区域农业产学研平台的发展现状来看,采用这一方式进行合作的主体主要为科研院所单位。总体来看,科研合作涉及的领域非常广。例如,中国内蒙古自治区农牧业科学院与蒙古国国立农业大学动物兽医学院联合开展"中蒙兽用天然药物资源挖掘与新药创制合作研究"项目,双方共同调研,对边境共有的

天然药物进行采集和试验；此外，双方互派专家指导对方团队，并积极鼓励团队成员进行交换交流，对天然药物资源使用后的效果进行长期监测并及时反馈，共同撰写计划申报材料，共同参与试验和数据整理，做到资源共享、成果共享。中国吉林省白城市农业科学院与俄罗斯联合开展"中俄特色农业国际联合实验室项目"，与俄罗斯国家科学院等多家科研机构进行农业科技合作，建立联合研究平台，推进两国农业关键领域的技术突破与创新，共同推进优异种质创新、技术整合升级，打造"中俄特色杂粮杂豆优势产区"和"中俄特色农业产品集散中心"。

除此之外，也有企业参与大图们区域农业产学研平台的构建中，并取得了较好的成效。例如，中国吉林省农业科学院近年来与俄罗斯农业科学院远东农业科学中心、中国吉林省金达海外农业开发投资有限公司等农业单位及科技企业共同合作，在俄罗斯远东地区开展了大豆、苜蓿等作物示范推广及乳品加工技术的农业交流与合作；与此同时，共同组建了中俄"远东农业科学研究中心"，开展了大豆、玉米、小麦、苜蓿、马铃薯等农作物生态学试验研究，其中在吉林省金达海外农业开发投资有限公司的海外农场进行了 100 公顷的公农 1 号紫花苜蓿品种试验示范，科研单位和企业共同努力，取得了较好的回报。中国内蒙古自治区特牧牧业开发有限公司积极参与到中国内蒙古自治区农牧业科学院与蒙古国农业科研单位的研究之中，并联合多家单位共同实施"中蒙抗寒水稻、大豆种植试验推广基地建设项目"，2016 年在蒙古国建设示范基地 100 公顷，完成高寒地区种植水稻 3 个品种、高寒地区大豆 3 个品种的种植初试工作。

（二）建设境外生产基地，实现多方互利共赢

涉农企业在原有业务的基础上，通过在境外流转土地等方式，建设

境外农业生产基地,借助于境内外资金、技术、人才、资源等互补优势,实现经济、社会、生态等多方面效益,为海内外的农业共同发展提供了动力。例如,绥芬河市宝国经贸有限责任公司是中国黑龙江省开展对俄农业合作十大企业之一,公司充分利用境内外两个市场、两种资源,不断延伸农业合作产业链和发展空间。公司在俄罗斯成立两家独资公司,经过多年的发展,已经形成集境外种植、养殖、保税加工于一体的完整跨境农业产业布局。俄罗斯北方农业公司是在俄罗斯成立的中资独资公司,该公司从俄罗斯下列区政府和比罗比詹区政府及其他俄罗斯农业公司租有农业用地 20000 多公顷,累计投资 6000 多万元人民币,投资修建了水利及其配套设施、烘干塔、地秤等,目前已开垦荒地 15000 公顷,并种植了大豆、水稻、玉米等农作物,年产粮食 4 万余吨。该项目的建设与实施,极大地推动了当地农业产业的发展,通过荒地开垦和基础设施建设,对当地种植业的长远发展具有重要意义。此外,该项目也在传统种植业的基础上进一步发展农产品初级加工业,不断提升和深化农业产业,带动诸如仓储物流等产业发展,从整体上实现区域经济协同推进。

(三)创办境外集散中心,丰富当地产品市场

涉农企业通过在境外建立冷库仓储中心、配送中心等方式,进一步连接境内生产基地与境外市场,实现区域资源和市场互补,最终有效实现境内外供需对接。例如,中国辽宁省主要从事果品收购、储存、销售、加工业务的沈阳威云果品有限公司目前正在俄罗斯后贝加尔边疆区建设 2 万吨冷藏库项目,占地面积达 2 万平方米,通过境外仓储物流库建设,可以完成中国辽宁省各种果蔬产品在俄罗斯当地的分装,项目的实施一方面进一步树立了中国辽宁农产品的品牌形象,另一方面也解决

了俄罗斯边疆区水果等农产品本地供给不足的问题。中国内蒙古自治区满洲里市德丰贸易有限责任公司投资 500 余万元建设跨境农产品分拨配送中心,一方面促进了菜农果农增产增收,另一方面解决了由于俄罗斯冬季寒冷漫长而导致的农产品市场存在较大缺口、储存不当造成果蔬类农产品冻害损失严重等问题。中国辽宁省沈阳俄中商贸有限公司在莫斯科国际食品城建立"辽宁中国名优商品展示中心",主要销售桦树茸产品、西红柿、彩椒、胡萝卜以及花卉等产品,丰富了当地产品市场。

三、大图们区域农业合作取得的成效

自大图们倡议提出以来,尤其是 2016 年农业委员会成立以来,成员方之间在农业方面的合作程度逐步加强,合作范围也逐步扩展,各方在经济、社会、生态等多个方面均实现了互惠共赢。总体来看,大图们区域的农业合作所取得的成效具体体现在以下几个方面。

(一)区域农业实现共同发展

大图们区域所包含的地理范围较为广泛,各成员方在资源、制度、科技、市场等多个方面均存在一定的差异,区域农业合作将弥补多方之间的不足,进而实现区域农业的共同发展。以中国的东北地区和俄罗斯的远东地区为例,两地在农业生产和农作物种植上有很多类似之处。俄罗斯土地资源丰富,人口少,种植粗放,在建立农业种植结构优化上尚未形成科技支撑体系,也没有形成当地农业的发展优势以及国际竞争力;中国在资源禀赋等方面存在较大的弱势,但在资金等方面具有一定的保障,双方的共同合作必然会形成各自的农业发展优势区,带动整个区域农业综合生产能力的提高。此外,中俄双方农业科研单位的合作研究,研究方向也不仅仅局限于种植,相关的加工及产业化成果将通过转化,带动特色农业产业的进步,也将拉动双方企业共同参与,促进共同联合,形成以加工成果为纽带、联合生产基地为支撑、企业联合集群为动力、开发系列特色产品为目标的中俄特色农业经济联系体系。

(二)科技合作取得重大成就

当前,大图们倡议成员方之间在农业科技方面的合作,在一些关键领域取得了重大突破,这一方面解决了农产品种植与各自区域生态特点结合不强的问题,另一方面也进一步深化了各方在农业科技方面的支撑体系。例如,自2003年起,中国吉林省白城市农业科学院就与俄罗斯多家农业科学院建立了广泛的合作与交流,先后与俄罗斯科学院东北区域农业科研所、萨马拉农业科研所、全俄谷类与豆类作物研究所、鞑靼农业科研所、全俄饲料研究所、乌拉尔农业研究所、伊尔库茨克农业研究所达成科技合作协议,在燕麦、冬黑麦、荞麦、马铃薯、豌豆等作物良种选育、栽培和加工技术等领域开展合作,取得了令双方满意的合作成果。中俄科学家合作育成的首个冬黑麦新品种"白BK01"的大面积推广,对中俄黑麦新产品研发、加工工艺创新、生态环境保护、特色产业升级、中俄贸易途径拓展产生了深远的影响。

(三)区域生态环境得以改善

大图们区域不同单位之间的相互合作,尤其是在农业科技研发和推广领域的相互合作,进一步改善了区域内的生态环境状况,为整个区域的健康可持续发展奠定了较好的基础。例如,中国内蒙古自治区农牧业科学院与蒙古国合作开展的"中蒙兽用天然药物资源挖掘与新药创制合作研究"项目,能够使养殖业更加适应现代化生产及禁牧舍饲的要求,有效地减少草原过载的压力,对维护草场、防止沙化、涵养水分、保护生态平衡和可持续发展将起到积极的建设性的作用,实现了生产生态双赢。该院与俄罗斯合作开展的"'三化'土地种植的菊芋优质高产高效种植模式及技术措施"项目,对治理由盐碱化、沙漠化和荒漠化引发的风沙暴等问题具有重要的推动作用,对于改善生态环境、促进节能减排、实现低碳经济均具有重大意义。

(四)地域就业难题得以解决

当前,大图们区域之间的农业合作领域呈现多样化的趋势,为投资区域的农业经济发展带来了活力,与此同时,通过大图们倡议成员方之间的农业合作,尤其是通过农业境外投资的方式进行农业合作,为当地带来了大量的就业岗位,解决了就业难的问题。例如,中国黑龙江省绥芬河市宝国经贸有限责任公司在俄罗斯所投资建立的伊列娜有限责任公司和绿色田野有限责任公司共拥有员工147人,其中,俄方员工84人。中国吉林省吉蒙农牧产业发展有限公司在蒙古国所开展的"吉蒙生态农牧产业国际合作园"项目,目前雇用当地牧民55人,未来项目完成后将带动350户牧民共同致富。中国在俄罗斯成立的北方农业公司,目前拥有由9名俄罗斯员工组成的管理团队,团队成员具有法律、财务、税收和农业机械技术等多方面专业知识,并从俄罗斯当地雇用工人100余人。

(五)农业产业共同转型升级

各方在农业领域的合作并不局限于传统的种植业和养殖业,而是在传统产业上进一步扩展,在涉农产品领域建立生产加工基地,将传统的农业产业进行升级改造,不断延伸农业产业链条,各方共同实现互利共赢。中国辽宁省禾丰牧业股份有限公司与俄方在俄罗斯远东滨海边疆区联合成立俄罗斯禾丰牧业有限公司,项目总投资金额2800万元人民币,其中,辽宁禾丰牧业股份有限公司投资1540万人民币,占55%的股份;俄方以生物资产投资,投资总额为1260万元人民币,占45%的股份。该项目除了进行传统的家禽、牲畜饲养业务之外,还将开展饲料及饲料添加剂生产、加工、销售、收购及贸易等业务,不断推动产业转型升级,项目的实施将会推动中俄双方实现更大收益,也同时为该区域创造更多的就业岗位。

四、大图们区域农业合作的未来展望

未来农业合作应立足于农业科技的深度合作,不断拓展农业产业链条,推动各方企业深化农业合作,并大力推动农业贸易往来,实现大图们区域农业的共同发展。

(一)共同谋划,谱写大图们区域农业合作新篇章

随着"一带一路"建设的持续推进,中国与周边国家的合作越来越紧密,同时越来越多的国家也加入进来,形成了新的格局。大图们区域是"一带一路"北线的重要区域,沿线国家和地区的民生福祉不断提升,农业发展也正在向高质量推进。农业领域作为区域合作的重要组成部分,未来将在大图们区域成员方的共同发展过程中扮演重要角色。因此,未来成员方之间应不断巩固多方互利合作,在农业科技发展、食

品安全、农产品贸易、农业农村开发等领域不断深化合作,共同形成内外联动、多向互济的开放格局,共同谱写大图们区域农业合作新篇章。

(二)共同建设,实现大图们区域农业合作新发展

大图们区域涉及的国家在资源禀赋、经济发展、政治环境等方面均有所不同,不同国家在农业发展过程中的诉求具有一定的差异;不过大图们倡议作为一个具有包容性、开放性、全局性的国际合作机制,多方之间的共同合作将会推动区域协同发展。在今后的农业合作过程中,各成员方应充分立足区域农业优势,充分利用各方市场和资源,把坚持农业合作开放作为基本方向,在现有合作的基础上进一步拓展农业产业链条,深化农业产业上、中、下游的合作与发展,不断加强多双边农业国际交流合作,更好地为区域农业和农村经济发展服务。此外,应继续注重农业贸易往来,用国际贸易实现区域优势互补。针对大图们区域内市场的不同,继续推动农业博览会等重大农产品展洽会的组织和实施,并以此为契机搭建区域内企业洽谈平台,推动区域内具有地域特色的农产品不断拓展境外市场,提高本地农产品的影响力和知名度,拓宽农产品进出口渠道,大力促进农业贸易健康发展,以此形成区域优势互补。

(三)共享成果,开创大图们区域农业合作新局面

在未来农业合作过程中,应立足于农业科技的深度合作,不断拓展农业产业链条,推动区域内企业深化农业合作,并大力推动农业贸易往来,不断分享多双边在农业合作过程中所取得的经验,共享农业合作成果,以此实现大图们区域农业的共同发展。尤其是在农业科技领域,各成员方应进一步深化多方之间的合作机制,共享农业合作成果,用科技

力量推动区域农业发展。应继续依托科研院所、创新型企业和科技中介组织,建立农业技术交流合作服务平台,加强农业科技交流合作,深化多双边在农作物种质资源开发利用、作物栽培育种技术、植物保护等领域合作,推动各方科研单位联合实验室共建、示范基地共建等多种模式,积极搭建产学研平台,促进产学研一体化,用科技力量推动区域农业发展。

科技研发篇

案 例 一

中蒙兽用天然药物资源
挖掘与新药创制合作研究项目

◇◆◇◆◇◆◇◆◇◆◇◆◇◆◇◆◇◆◇◆◇◆◇◆◇◆◇◆◇◆◇◆◇◆◇◆

一、合作概览

(一)总体情况

自 2017 年开始,中国内蒙古自治区农牧业科学院兽医研究所与蒙古国国立农业大学动物兽医学院(见图 1-1)共同合作,双方开展"中蒙兽用天然药物资源挖掘与新药创制合作研究项目"。

双方开展的工作如下:

将内蒙古自治区丰富的天然药物资源与蒙古国大规模的牛羊试验基地相结合;开展天然矿物药物,如稀土、腐植酸钠以及重点蒙药材的研究;对天然药物有效活性成分进行分离、提取和纯化;开展药理药效学试验、药代动力学试验和药物安全性试验;建立质量标准,完善生产工艺;开发蒙兽药新制剂。

研究成果通过推广应用于中蒙两国大型牧场。

发挥其抗菌、抗寄生虫、抗炎和免疫的综合药理作用;宣传绿色健康的养殖理念,培训专业知识丰富的科技人员和当地农户,提高中蒙双方对动物疫病的防控,促进畜牧业健康绿色发展。

图 1-1 蒙古国国立农业大学动物兽医学院

图片来源:中国内蒙古农牧业科学院兽医研究所。

(二)合作价值

解决中蒙双方动物疫病防控的关键性问题;积极推动中蒙联合研究项目、联合实验室等科技创新合作;促进人员交流与培训。

通过项目建设,不断深化中蒙两国科技创新合作,增加农牧民的经济收入,促进畜牧业健康绿色发展,进而增加农业经济产值,助力蒙古国经济和社会发展。

二、合作实施

（一）完成项目

2017 年，中国内蒙古自治区农牧业科学院兽医研究所和蒙古国立农业大学就合作开展"中蒙兽用天然药物资源挖掘与新药创制合作研究项目"签订科研合作协议；双方对试验条件环境和动物试验基地开展了调研；2017 年 11 月，双方就"中蒙兽用天然药物资源挖掘与新药创制合作研究项目"合作申报了 2018 年度中国国家重点研发计划——政府间国际科技创新合作重点专项，当年通过了中国科技部立项审批并获得资助。

该项目实施以来，中蒙双方均发挥各自的地域优势，双方项目均按期进展顺利。

（二）进行中项目

该项目由中蒙双方共同致力于收集传统蒙古族兽医药方制剂，掌握蒙兽医药的传统制作工艺，同时对尚未发掘的常见天然兽药制品进行再开发利用，创制出新型、绿色、健康、高效的兽医生物制剂，是双方在该领域的首次尝试。

目前正在进行的项目有：

筛选 5—8 种植物源性天然药物（瑞香狼毒、狼毒、石榴皮、黄芪、蜘蛛香、黄芩、小白蒿、红豆草）和矿物源性天然药物稀土以及腐植酸钠；制定新兽药质量标准和适用于两国的生产技术规程；完成蒙兽药新产品的研发;将蒙兽药新试剂示范应用于蒙古国多个牛羊养殖场,使动物疾病发生率降低,饲料利用率明显提高。

(三)下一步工作

下一步,双方将继续完成项目内容和签订的科研合作协议内容,并加强合作,巩固合作成果。

三、合作特色

(一)合作效益

中蒙两国在推进"一带一路"科技创新合作方面具有共识;充分发挥了政府间科技合作联委会机制的统筹协调作用;积极推动了蒙古国科技联合研究项目、联合实验室、技术转移中心等科技创新合作。

此外,该项目的实施也能够促成双方对自然资源的有序开发和利用,使畜牧业生产方式由数量扩张型逐渐转入质量效益型阶段,使养殖业更能适应现代化生产及禁牧舍饲的要求,有效地减轻草原过载的压力,对维护草场、防止沙化、涵养水分、保护生态平衡和可持续发展将起到建设性作用,实现生产生态双赢。

(二)合作空间

该项目的合作领域较为广泛,双方在共同合作过程中涉及多个方面,图1-2展示了双方之间的合作空间。

```
┌─────────────────────────────────────────────┐
│   中蒙兽用天然药物资源挖掘与新药创制合作研究   │
└─────────────────────────────────────────────┘
```

| 天然药物的筛选 | 天然药物有效活性成分的研究 | 天然药物制剂的研究 |

资源分布、储量和生态状况，药性、炮制方法、主治、功能等

天然药物有效成分（黄酮、多糖、生物碱、脂肪酸和元素）的提取分离

天然药物有效成分抗菌方面的研究

天然药物有效成分对小鼠抗炎免疫的影响

天然药物有效成分抗寄生虫方面的研究

天然药物制剂的组成与配比

安全性评估试验

加工工艺流程和生产技术规范

对动物机体各指标的影响

推广与应用

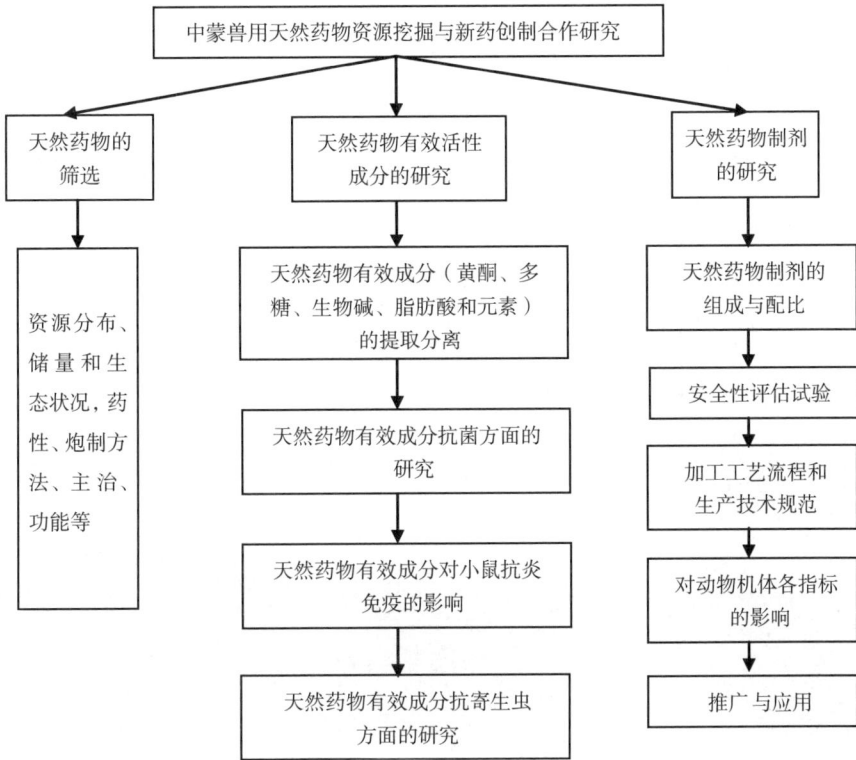

图1-2 中蒙兽用天然药物资源挖掘与新药创制合作研究示意图

（三）示范效应

该项目的开展对其他农业主体开展农业合作具有较强的示范带动作用。

一方面，该项目具有较强的创新性。一是天然药物资源配比在中国尚属首次，资源配比药效覆盖面广，对细菌、病毒和寄生虫等多种病原均有良好的抑制效果及治疗作用。二是开发草场上有毒杂草作为植物源性天然药物来源进行研究，如瑞香狼毒，作为北方草地常见的有毒杂草之一，随着其种群数量逐年增加，在局部地区甚至形成优势植物群

落,导致草场退化,严重影响畜牧业生产。

另一方面,该项目具有较强的先进性。一是开展以现代药学研究为基础的有毒杂草新兽药研究可以充分利用其药用价值,又能抑制有毒杂草繁殖蔓延,控制草场退化,保护草原生态环境,合理利用自然资源,变害为宝。二是临床上长期滥用抗生素类药物,许多病原产生抗药性后,抗生素用药量不断加大,且较难治愈,随之而来产生的毒副作用也越加严重,所以找到抗生素的替代品,既可以治疗动物疫病,又绿色环保,能够减少耐药菌株的出现等。

案 例 二

韩国国际农业合作蒙古国中心项目

◇◇◇

一、综　述

（一）韩国国际农业合作蒙古国中心

成立日期:2014 年 2 月 16 日(韩国政府与蒙古国政府签订谅解备忘录:2013 年 12 月 23 日)。

地点:蒙古国生命科学大学(MULS)畜牧业研究所 4 层。

目的:开展合作项目,开发和推广适合蒙古国环境的农业技术。

目标区域:涉及 3 个省份[TUV 省乌兰巴托(Ulaanbaatar)、色楞格省(Selenge)、布尔干省（Bulgan）]的 12 个地区。

（二）蒙古国境内合作机构

食品、农业与轻工业部:国家农业推广中心。

教育文化科学体育部:农业科学研究院植物保护研究所、蒙古国生命科学大学、畜牧研究所。

二、合作实施(自 2014 年起)

1. 整体进度:已完成项目有 5 项,进行中项目有 5 项。具体项目开展情况如图 2-1 所示。

2. 已完成项目:5 个项目,2014—2018 年共投入资金 59.2 万美元(见表 2-1)。

表 2-1　已完成项目概况

项目名称	项目周期
小麦良种繁育及新品种培育试点	2014—2017 年
饲用作物(苜蓿)良种繁育试点	2014—2017 年
采用粗饲料和强化营养提高羔羊和羊毛产量和遗传价值	2014—2017 年
建立农业科研、培训和生产示范农场	2015—2018 年
农民及农业推广人员教育计划	2015—2017 年

3. 进行中项目:5 个项目,2019 年共投入资金 19 万美元(见表 2-2)。

表 2-2　进行中项目概况

项目名称	项目周期
(开发)适应蒙古国环境的韩国洋葱品种的选择与分布	2018—2020 年
(开发)选择和推广适应蒙古国环境的韩国番茄品种	2018—2020 年
(开发)制定规范化技术,提高蒙古国肉牛产量	2018—2020 年
(开发)适应蒙古国环境的多年生牧草品种种子繁殖与分配	2019—2022 年
(示范)蒙古国小麦良种繁育和蒙古族注册品种生产试点	2017—2019 年

（1）优种Darkhan166, 144	（2）优种Darkhan–131, 34	（3）出版材料
（4）露天种植苜蓿	（5）新闻报道	（6）洋葱品种
（7）Belkh地区农场	（8）冬季的农场内温室	（9）玉米收获
（10）土豆栽培	（11）选择牛进行测试	（12）饲料

| （13）检测中心 | （14）受试动物 |

图 2-1　项目开展情况

三、主要成就及特点

（一）提高作物生产力

优良小麦品种的繁殖和分布。适合蒙古国环境的 4 个注册品种的产量达每公顷 287 吨,相当于生产力提高了 38.8%;并计划于 2019 年生产 2000 吨注册种子。

传播实地经验技术。传播旨在建立蔬菜种植试点农场和建立示范农场,或传播农业研究、培训和生产技术。

确认韩国蔬菜是否适应蒙古国环境。涉及 5 个樱桃番茄品种,5 个洋葱品种,以及大白菜、生菜、萝卜等 8 种作物;并推广育苗技术(嫁接技术)和灌溉技术,改善土壤肥力。

（二）提高畜牧业生产力

改进规格技术,提升遗传价值。建立轮牧制度,冬季采用 3 种饲养方式;开发30公顷草地用于轮牧,利润增加290000图格里克/肉牛。通过提供人工受精技术提高羔羊和羊毛的生产力。

四、现有问题

一是缺乏适合蒙古国环境的蔬菜和饲料作物栽培的优化技术。例如,缺乏可在蒙古国种植的选定品种的栽培技术(樱桃番茄、洋葱);需要改善可持续饲料喂养计划的系统化。二是缺乏适合蒙古国环境的专业人员和农业教育材料。

五、预期计划

(一)改进技术和农业生产力以适应蒙古国环境

采用系统化技术在环境可控设施中种植作物,并在农场进行试验:在5个樱桃番茄农场、2个洋葱农场开展测试;生产100吨优质小麦种苗,蔬菜产量提高10%—15%;设定合理饲喂标准,稳定冬季牲畜管理。

(二)加强农业技术交流和教育

发布2份农业技术报告,开展3项农民教育项目(90人)。开展蒙古国科研人员专业培训计划:培养4名饲草饲喂专家。由韩国农村振兴厅(RDA)派出6名专家提供现场咨询,领域包括洋葱、小麦、土壤管理、饲料。

六、详细情况

2014—2018 年,通过不同的培训项目共培训 3144 人(见表 2-3)。

表 2-3　项目培训人数统计表

培训人数＼年份	2014	2015	2016	2017	2018	总计
RDA 培训	5	25	—	—	7	37
专家培训	2	18	1	3	6	30
全球培训项目	4	5	5	5	5	24
农民农业教育	—	642	770	1233	408	3053
总计	—	—	—	—	—	3144

案 例 三

中俄大豆、苜蓿品种示范
推广及乳品加工技术合作项目

❖❖❖❖❖❖❖❖❖❖❖❖❖❖❖❖❖❖❖❖❖❖❖❖❖❖❖❖❖❖❖❖❖❖

一、合作概览

（一）总体情况

中国吉林省农业科学院近年来先后与俄罗斯农业单位及中国科技企业进行合作,在俄罗斯远东地区开展了大豆、苜蓿等作物示范推广及乳品加工技术的农业交流与合作。开展合作的单位及企业有:俄罗斯农业科学院远东科学中心、俄罗斯滨海农业研究所、俄罗斯远东农业研究所、俄罗斯滨海农业公司、中国吉林省金达海外农业开发投资有限公司及其子公司俄罗斯土星公司。

此外,中方与俄方还共同组建了中俄"远东农业科学研究中心",开展了大豆、玉米、小麦、苜蓿、马铃薯等农作物生态学试验研究,以及乳酸菌菌种资源的收集整理和建立跨区域乳酸菌菌种资源库等工作。

（二）合作价值

该项目的开展，一方面将促使俄罗斯成为向中国及亚洲国家出口粮食和肉类制品的重要基地。另一方面，该项目为中国吉林省在俄罗斯远东地区发展农业和养殖业提供了巨大潜力空间。

按照"农业开发技术先行，先试验、后中试、再推广"的原则开展合作，发挥了中国吉林省农业科学院动植物品种选育、栽培、农机技术、畜牧养殖及农产品加工优势，同时面对企业和投资公司拥有资金却缺少技术的情况，为众多农业企业开展对外合作提供有力的农业技术支撑。

二、合作实施

（一）完成和进行中项目

目前，多方共同开展以下几个方面的合作。

1. 优质大豆品种在俄罗斯远东地区筛选、试种、推广

中国吉林省农业科学院与吉林省金达海外农业开发投资有限公司开展合作，筛选大豆优良品种6份（吉育202、吉育204等），在吉林省金达海外农业开发投资有限公司（子公司俄罗斯土星公司）农场进行了推广试种，筛选的6个品种均适合在俄罗斯远东地区种植、推广。

2. 苜蓿品种在俄罗斯远东地区筛选、试种、推广

2018年，中国吉林省农业科学院与俄罗斯滨海农业研究所、吉林省金达海外农业开发投资有限公司子公司——俄罗斯土星公司签订了

苜蓿品种比较试验合同,制订了苜蓿品种比较试验方案,试验选用双方各3个,共计6个紫花苜蓿品种。

3. 益生菌和发酵乳制品加工技术示范推广和产品开发

双方共同开展了中国东北地区和俄罗斯远东地区乳酸菌菌种资源的收集整理和建立跨区域乳酸菌菌种资源库工作。

在俄罗斯远东地区采集传统发酵乳制品、酸黄瓜等发酵果蔬产品260余份。利用本实验室乳酸菌分离鉴定方法和技术,从样品中分离出乳酸菌新菌株390株,其中乳杆菌320株、乳球菌70株,对这些菌株进行了编号和保藏,并对菌株的发酵特性和益生特性进行了评价。

此外还开展益生菌加工制备技术在俄罗斯远东地区的示范推广及应用研究,开发系列益生菌发酵乳制品,如酸奶、奶酪等新产品(见图3-1)。

4. 中俄远东地区农业科学研究中心建设

中国吉林省农业科学院和俄罗斯远东农业研究所共同组建的“远东农业科学研究中心”,于2018年11月1日在俄罗斯哈巴罗夫斯克正式举行了合作签约和揭牌仪式,双方旨在进行大豆、苜蓿、禾谷类作物引种试验以及畜牧养殖、农产品加工等领域的技术交流。

(二)下一步工作

中国吉林省农业科学院与俄罗斯远东地区在以上四项内容的合作正在有序进行中,在中俄远东地区农业科学研究中心的基础上,双方继续围绕“优质大豆品种在俄罗斯远东地区筛选、试种、推广”“苜蓿品种在俄罗斯远东地区筛选、试种、推广”“益生菌和发酵乳制品加工技术示范推广和产品开发”这几项内容展开研究。在未来发展过程中,双方期待在这三个领域的技术研发中能够取得突破。

（1）菌种保藏图片

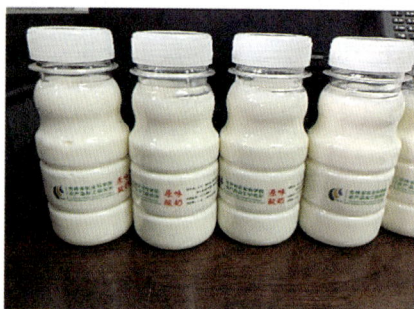

（2）益生菌酸奶新产品

（3）切达奶酪新产品

图 3-1 项目生产的益生菌及发酵乳产品

图片来源:项目中方执行单位。

三、合作特色

（一）合作效益

通过合作,双方在经济、社会、生态方面均取得了一定的效益。

经济效益方面,中国吉林省农业科学院与吉林省金达海外农业开发投资有限公司(子公司俄罗斯土星公司)合作,共筛选大豆优良品种

6份,在俄罗斯远东地区推广种植面积3.6万亩,大豆销售收入2100万元;完成了抗寒、高产苜蓿品种在俄罗斯远东地区试种1500亩,其中春播550亩,第一年亩产0.5吨,苜蓿草销售收入66万元。

社会效益方面,为俄罗斯远东地区收集乳酸菌菌种资源260余份,分离鉴定乳酸菌新菌株390株,完成了乳酸菌和发酵乳制品加工技术推广。建立了区域农业研究中心——中国吉林省农业科学院俄罗斯远东农业研究所农业科学研究中心,建立联合共建实验室1个,开展农业对外合作科技人才的交流和培养等。

在生态效益方面,苜蓿草种植选择山坡荒地连片种植,一次种植可连续生长收割6—8年,苜蓿发达的根部对土壤、水分起到保护作用,增强地表植被覆盖能力,有效防止水土流失,治理土地沙化,对生态环境的改善作用十分显著。

(二)合作空间

2018年9月在俄罗斯乌苏里斯克市举办的远东农工综合体:科学成果国际会议上,中国吉林省农业科学院先后作了"中国吉林省农科院牧草育种研究进展""中国吉林省农科院大豆遗传育种研究进展""中国吉林省生物防治现状及前景"等专题报告,双方进一步落实已签署合作协议内容,对远东滨海农业研究所、吉林省金达海外农业开发投资有限公司的苜蓿品种比较试验和示范,以及在试验数据采集、调研、农作物植物保护技术交流等方面进一步达成协议。

(三)示范效应

该项目的开展具有一定的代表性,其中最重要的示范效应主要表现在产学研平台搭建上。科研机构通过与外方科研机构进行合作,并借助于境内机构在外方所创办的农业企业,有效建立起产学研平台,在逐步推进农业科学研发的同时,也不断进行农产品的试验和推广,产学研平台的搭建有效实现了科研与市场相结合,既提升了农业科研单位在共同合作过程中的积极性,也进一步加强了双方农业市场的协同发展。

案 例 四

中蒙沼气技术与农村能源、环境保护培训班项目

◇◇◇◇◇◇◇◇◇◇◇◇◇◇◇◇◇◇◇◇◇◇◇◇◇◇◇◇◇◇◇◇◇◇

一、合作概览

2019 年 6 月 28 日至 8 月 16 日,中国农业农村部沼气科学研究所
(BIOMA)举办了为期 45 天的"沼气技术与农村能源、环境保护"培
训班。

本次培训在成都举办,来自蒙古国、埃塞俄比亚、阿富汗、墨西哥、
萨摩亚、利比亚、南苏丹、加纳、安提瓜和几内亚等十余个发展中国家的
24 位代表参加了本次培训,学习沼气技术。

其中共有 4 位来自蒙古国的学员,包括蒙古国商品交易所战略分
析部门专家,蒙古国省中部畜牧草场使用管理委员会专家,蒙古国兽医
监督总局国家食品安全参考、实验室专家以及蒙古国社会保障监察机
构卫生部相关专家。

二、合作实施

本次培训主要包括 3 项主要内容。

(一)课堂培训

课堂培训包括 126 学时的理论课,共计 21 轮。

理论课由经验丰富的教授授课,传授专业知识,如沼气技术的开发、沼气发酵微生物学、废物利用、大中型企业沼气生产发酵、新型建筑材料和新型沼气技术、在干燥空气环境中引进消化技术等。

(二)实验室培训

实验室培训分为微生物实验室和中央工程实验室两部分。

实验室培训时长共计 6 天 36 小时,主要进行研究分析,包括硅胶层析法、微生物多样性、甲烷菌培养的无空气环境、沼气发酵原料实验 TS/VS、沼气中甲烷成分的简单分析等。

(三)技术与实践培训

生物反应器建设公司参加了为期 5 天的建设实训;成都安美科燃气技术股份有限公司参与了荣州市沼气检测项目;成都顺美国际贸易有限公司和德阳沼气共同介绍了利用沼气清洁养鸡场的项目(见图 4-1)。

（1）当地排水系统的解决方法　　　　　　（2）Munkhnasan参与生物反应器建设工作

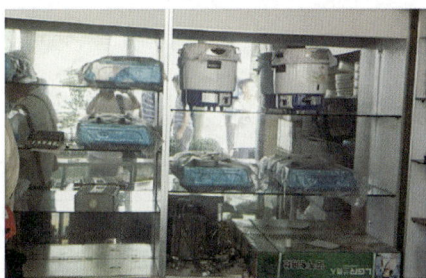

（3）使用沼气的家用电器　　　　　　　　　（4）当地能源

图4-1　技术与实践培训场景

图片来源：项目中方执行单位。

三、合作效益

蒙古国共4位学员参加了发展中国家沼气技术与农村能源、环境保护培训课程，并顺利结业。

蒙古国尚无能力发展农村能源和相关环境保护的技术，通过一次培训，有助于蒙古国充分利用当地能源、农业废料、电力和供水以及非化学肥料，实施推广沼气技术。

案 例 五

中韩农业科技合作项目

◇◇◇

一、项目概况

周期和预算:1995 年至今,129 万美元。

目标区域:中华人民共和国。

实施机构:韩国农村振兴厅;中国农业科学院。

二、合作历程

1994 年 4 月 9 日,韩国农村振兴厅与中国农业科学院达成农业科技合作谅解备忘录;在双方都关注的领域进行联合研究。

2001 年 4 月 19 日,韩国农村振兴厅派遣官员到中国农业科学院。

2015 年 12 月 11 日,双方在中国农业科学院建立联合研究实验室。

三、主要成就

（一）农业科技合作项目与交流

1. 联合研究和专家人员交流（1995年至今）

进行联合研究：共89个领域，涵盖农作物培植、培育、基因资源等；专家人员通过联合科研与交流项目进行沟通，共有700名研究人员。

2. 建立联合实验室，派遣韩国研究人员到华

探索合作项目，促进双方沟通，收集并分析中方农业科技数据；自2001年起，已派遣过9名研究人员；已派遣第9组研究人员（周期：2018年4月—2020年2月）。

（二）学术研究成果共享

1. 举办过22次农业科技合作战略论坛（1995年至今）

（1）共享学术成果，探索新项目；（2）为推动合作关系进行磋商，促进项目发展。

2. 举办过4次韩中药用植物中长期国际化战略研讨会（2015年至今）

共同努力，促进药用植物国际标准化，增进合作。

（三）主要成就

通过与特种动植物研究所（ISAPS）合作，在全球范围内首次制定中药五味子种子和种苗国际标准（ISO19824—2017），为促进五味子种

子种苗的国际贸易奠定基础。

四、未来布局

2020 年,在韩国全州举办第 23 届农业科技合作战略论坛。分享合作项目成果,探索新的项目合作机遇,为促进双边合作展开磋商。

案 例 六
中蒙抗寒水稻、大豆种植试验示范推广项目

◇◇

一、合作概览

（一）总体情况

2015 年,中国内蒙古自治区兴安盟科右中旗特牧牧业开发有限公司与蒙古国 Bornuur Ecofoods 公司（蒙古国中央省）、蒙古国沃土有限责任公司（蒙古国鄂尔浑省）共同确立了中蒙抗寒水稻、大豆种植示范推广项目（见图 6-1）。

该项目以中国内蒙古自治区兴安盟科右中旗特牧牧业开发有限公司为项目主持单位,蒙古国两公司参与项目之中并提供土地及附属设施。

（二）合作价值

本项目的价值主要体现在三个方面。

（1）水稻种植　　　　　　　　　　　　　（2）大豆种植

图 6-1　抗寒水稻、大豆种植

图片来源：项目中方执行单位

第一，填补了蒙古国水稻、大豆种植生产的空白。通过项目实施，可以实现大豆机械化作业和大面积种植。

第二，蒙古国是传统畜牧业国家，农业特别是经济作物种植领域相对落后，随着集约化畜牧业的发展，青贮玉米的大量种植将解决牲畜冬季饲补问题，保障牲畜安全越冬。

第三，通过帮助建立合作社，宣传了中国的先进技术；通过各种途径的培训，提高了当地农牧民的认知度，解决了农牧民实际困难，得到了农牧民的理解和接纳，并最终得到了蒙古国各界的统一认识。

二、合作实施

（一）完成项目

该项目自 2016 年开始实施，2017—2018 年在蒙古国中央省和鄂尔浑省分别建设示范基地 10 公顷。

2018 年年底,项目完成了高寒地区水稻 3 个品种、大豆 3 个品种的种植初试工作;青贮玉米种植 45 公顷,收获 700 多吨,青贮玉米栽培管理技术基本成熟;并完成大豆和饲料玉米的成功种植。

(二)进行中项目

2019 年开始,该项目开始开展抗寒水稻和大豆在蒙古国不同地区的种植试验,预计投资 20 多万元。

(三)下一步工作

该项目下一步将进入中试阶段,具体工作内容如下。

将大豆种植面积扩展至 500 亩,水稻种植面积扩展至 100 亩。在不同地区种植试验,积累经验;其他作物也逐步扩大种植面积,将青贮玉米面积扩展至 5000 亩以上。

在蒙古国帮助组建合作社,尽可能得到牧民的认可和支持,拟组建 3 个合作社。

对蒙古国涉农领域的相关领导、学者和农牧民进行培训,计划培训次数 6 次,其中牧民培训人数 500 人次(妇女培训人数不少于 350 人次)。

举办国际、国内合作交流会议各 2 次。

大量吸纳在中国留学过的蒙古国留学生,组建项目团队,为进一步扩大项目影响力和日后项目的申报和执行奠定良好基础。

把试验成果在蒙古国中央省、色楞格省、达尔罕省、肯特省和科布多省 5 个省的多个县广泛推广,逐步扩大水稻、大豆、青贮玉米和饲料玉米的种植面积。

三、合作特色

（一）合作效益

目前该项目正处于试验阶段，整个项目处于起步阶段，尚未产生效益。但是，未来三年内该项目计划扩大种植面积，届时将会获得可观的收益。

水稻拟计划种植面积 1500 亩，亩产达到 400 公斤，预计销售收入达到 240 万元，纯收入应达到 120 万元；大豆拟计划种植面积 5000 亩，亩产达到 100 公斤，预计销售收入达到 260 万元，纯收入应达到 130 万元；青贮玉米拟计划种植 3000 亩，亩产达到 1500 公斤，预计销售收入应达到 120 万元，纯收入应达到 80 万元。

除了经济收益之外，该项目也可为当地提供一定的就业岗位：按照蒙古国就业政策，外国人与蒙古国人 1：9 的比例，该项目用人高峰期每个基地用人数量大约一百人以上。

（二）合作空间

未来可在两个方面继续拓展项目合作空间：一是继续拓展青贮和大豆的种植项目，并可开展秸秆利用项目，以此解决中蒙双方养殖业饲料短缺问题；二是将研究沙漠水稻生产技术项目，拓展新的研究和试验领域。

（三）示范效应

该项目通过进行调研宣传、试验种植和培训，在当地部分农民中形成示范效应,使得作物秸秆得到充分利用,同时,大豆、玉米饲料等作为冬季饲料,也为当地牲畜安全越冬提供了有力保障。

该项目将中国的技术引入蒙古国,并结合蒙古国的自然资源特点开展新的试验研究,为其他方面的农业技术开发与合作提供了示范。同时,双方相互利用各自优势,在优势互补的条件下实现互利共赢。

案 例 七

中蒙洗净山羊绒收购合作项目

◇◆◇◆◇◆◇◆◇◆◇◆◇◆◇◆◇◆◇◆◇◆◇◆◇◆◇◆◇◆◇◆◇◆◇◆◇

一、合作概览

（一）总体情况

中国内蒙古自治区维信羊绒集团建立于 1992 年,是集科研、牧业、工业、贸易于一体的跨国企业集团。企业主要生产和经营羊绒系列制品,年生产能力羊绒 2000 吨,羊绒纱 600 吨,羊绒衫 200 万件,羊绒围巾、披肩 200 万条,羊绒粗纺面料 50 万米,高档羊绒服装 8 万件。集团是"农业产业化国家重点龙头企业"、"中国羊绒行业十强企业"、商务部"AAA 信用企业"、国家质检总局"中国出口质量安全示范企业"、"出口纺织品一类企业"、海关总署"A 类企业"、国家"高新技术企业"。

中国内蒙古自治区维信羊绒集团与蒙古国宏聚有限责任公司经过双方友好协商,本着平等、互利、优势互补、诚信自愿的原则,达成以下协议:收购 500—1000 吨洗净山羊绒,项目总投资约 45000 万元人民币,到 2020 年年底完成。

(二)合作价值

蒙古国的绒山羊是特色家畜品种之一,拥有悠久的绒山羊饲养史,蒙古国是生产山羊绒的大国。山羊绒业是蒙古国的主要经济来源之一,蒙古国山羊绒产量大、市场价格低,是中国补充羊绒资源不足、羊绒进口的重要来源之一。

中国是羊绒资源第一大国,二狼山白山羊绒、阿尔巴斯白山羊绒、阿拉善白山羊绒以优良的品质享誉世界。中国也是羊绒制品生产第一大国,生产能力约占全球总量的 60%,在国际市场处于绝对垄断地位。但由于近年来生态环境的影响,制约了中国羊绒产业的发展。中蒙两国合作,将有助于实现优势互补,共同提升两国畜牧业和加工业的发展。

二、合作实施

(一)完成项目和进行中项目

2019 年 6 月 27 日,在中国内蒙古自治区—蒙古国经贸合作推介洽谈会上,中国内蒙古自治区维信羊绒集团与蒙古国宏聚有限责任公司达成 1000 吨洗净山羊绒收购协议。

中国内蒙古自治区维信羊绒集团与蒙古国宏聚有限责任公司将按照协议分别展开工作,推动项目进展;蒙方负责洗净山羊绒的收购、加工、检验、检疫、运输、出口报关手续等;中方负责筹集资金、验货接货。

(二)下一步工作

按照双方协议,2020 年 12 月 31 日前,中方募集资金 4.5 亿元,收购蒙古国洗净山羊绒 100 吨。

三、合作特色

(一)合作效益

双方合作刚处于达成意向阶段,尚未开展具体业务,未来双方合作预计将会取得可观的经济效益。

中蒙双方协议的签订,增进了相互理解和友好关系,切实维护了中蒙双方利益,确保双方合作共赢。通过技术改进和资金注入,进一步推动中蒙山羊绒产业的合作与发展。

(二)合作空间

蒙古国对畜牧业日益重视,按照《蒙古国政府行动规划 2016—2020》目标,将快速推进"蒙古国牲畜"计划,提升畜牧业经济效益,建立羊毛、羊绒和皮革收储与运输体系,为牲畜产品的加工与制造储备原料。

(三)示范效应

在蒙古国大力发展畜牧业及羊绒业的背景下,羊绒产业在第一产业中的比重会进一步增加。因而蒙古国洗净羊绒和分梳羊绒产量将获得稳定增长。

中国企业通过羊绒资源进口,在保护中国生态环境的同时,满足企业产能需求,进一步扩大羊绒针织制品的产量,提高羊绒产品的附加值与利润率,增加羊绒加工产品的出口额,这是中国羊绒产业今后发展的另一趋势。

中国内蒙古自治区维信羊绒集团与蒙古国宏聚有限责任公司1000吨洗净山羊绒项目的签订,深化了中蒙双方的经贸合作,为双方企业信息联通、优劣互补、合作共赢开辟了新思路。

案 例 八

中俄菊芋资源创新利用研究项目

一、合作概览

（一）总体情况

中国内蒙古自治区农牧业科学院与俄罗斯瓦维洛夫植物栽培研究所在菊芋资源领域开展合作研究。合作内容主要有：

菊芋品种资源选育技术、改良盐碱化、修复荒漠化、治理沙化地、菊芋饲料利用、新品种新技术示范六大关键技术研发；创建不同类型菊芋高产高效生态种植模式，制定模式建设标准；按模式各项技术规程建设修复盐碱化、荒漠化、沙化地、饲草料基地；应用模式集成的各项技术措施，以优良菊芋品种为基础，建设示范基地，带动内蒙古自治区能源植物原料基地的建设。

（二）合作价值

中国内蒙古自治区的菊芋资源拥有量少,盐碱化、沙漠化和荒漠化退化严重是直接影响京津风沙暴的源头,而能源植物菊芋是治理盐碱化、沙漠化和荒漠化退化引起风沙暴的最优良植物。中国内蒙古自治区可以利用菊芋解决土壤盐碱化、沙漠化和荒漠化退化的问题。此外,菊芋具有很强的耐寒耐旱能力,研究利用菊芋应对沙漠化等技术,也有助于解决生物质能源问题。

二、合作实施

（一）完成项目和进行中项目

目前,双方主要在以下四个方面开展项目合作。

1. 对菊芋资源创新、新品种选育及配套栽培技术研究

专用菊芋新品种引进和鉴定筛选;专用菊芋种质资源引进、鉴定、评价、繁种;专用菊芋种质资源创新与杂交组合选配。

2.“三化”土地种植菊芋新品种高产高效标准化栽培技术研究

盐碱化地种植菊芋新品种高产高效标准化栽培技术研究;荒漠化地种植菊芋新品种高产高效标准化栽培技术研究;沙化地种植菊芋新品种高产高效标准化栽培技术研究;编写菊芋高产高效栽培技术手册。

3. 菊芋饲草加工利用的研究

菊芋最晚刈割时间的研究;适宜青贮添加剂筛选;菊芋窖贮技术研究;菊芋青贮饲料消化率研究;菊芋青贮饲料利用方式和饲喂效果研究。

4. 菊芋综合技术集成与示范推广

在中国内蒙古自治区呼和浩特市托克托县、包头固阳县、乌兰察布市、鄂尔多斯市配合菊芋主产旗县进行科技推广示范。

（二）下一步工作

继续与俄罗斯互换菊芋资源材料，进行科技创新转化、示范园区建设、技术推广、种质资源培育等方面的合作。

三、合作特色

（一）合作效益

1. 经济效益

项目实施期间菊芋示范田增加收入502.5万元。通过品种改良和营养调控增加牛、羊产量和提高畜产品品质，可进一步提高牛、羊、猪、鸡、鸭养殖的经济效益。

2. 社会效益

就业人数增加、促进了地方科技突破和经济腾飞。

3. 生态效益

菊芋种植规模的扩大及种植技术的提高，有助于缓解土壤盐碱化、沙漠化和荒漠化等问题。

（二）合作空间

通过杂交等育种手段，将各种优良性状集于一体，并通过多年、多代的田间选择优良个体,选育出理想的符合育种目标的菊芋新品种。

对通过审定的科尔沁菊芋、蒙芋 2 号两个菊芋新品种和引进的菊芋新品种,进一步配套完善"三化"壤的高产高效栽培技术规程 2—3 个。

(三)示范效应

该项目通过两国科研合作的形式开展新品种研究,通过试验、示范在境内进行大面积推广。双方在科技方面的研究,加强了技术交流和合作,也为今后进一步扩大农业合作奠定了良好基础。此外,本项目所选取的研究品种具有一定的多功能性,研究成果除了具有一定的经济效益之外,更重要的是能够形成生态效应,对今后两国在生态环境方面的加强合作起到较好的示范作用。

案 例 九

中俄特色农业国际联合实验室项目

◇◆

一、合作概览

（一）总体情况

中国吉林省白城市农科院地处吉林西部,与俄罗斯农业发展地区如基诺夫、萨马拉等地在地缘上相近,在生态条件、农作物种植上具有许多共同点,为建立国际联合实验室及今后的成果共享创造了良好的先决条件。

2017 年 11 月,中国吉林省白城市农业科学院与俄罗斯科学院举行会谈,进一步加强谷类和牧草作物病害防治、种植栽培和加工技术的合作研究,依托吉林省白城市农业科学院国家国际科技合作基地和俄罗斯科学院东北区域农业科学中心已经搭建的合作平台,组建"中俄联合实验室",整合中俄双方谷类作物和其他农业优势领域专家,开展中俄农业科技创新合作,并签署了"建立中俄谷类作物育种栽培与加工技术中心"谅解备忘录。

(二)合作价值

在中俄农业合作的大背景下,通过与以俄罗斯国家科学院为首的多家俄罗斯农业科研机构开展农业科技合作,建立联合研究平台;推进两国特色农作物新品种选育、高效栽培技术集成、特色农产品加工利用等关键领域的技术交流与合作创新,共同推进优异种质创新、技术整合升级;广泛进行人才交流、农业特异资源交流和科技资源共享,全面拓展合作领域,进行特色产业推进,联合打造具有国际领先水平的特色农业产业;打造"中俄特色杂粮杂豆优势产区"和"中俄特色农业产品集散中心",促进国际贸易发展、高级人才联合培养,双边友谊互信的国际合作,带动中俄及周边国家农业贸易往来。

二、合作实施

(一)完成项目和进行中项目

自 2003 年起,中国吉林省白城市农业科学院就与俄罗斯多家农业科学院建立了广泛的合作与交流,先后与俄罗斯科学院东北区域农业科研所、萨马拉农业科研所、全俄谷类与豆类作物研究所、鞑靼农业科研所、全俄饲料研究所、乌拉尔农业研究所、伊尔库茨克农业研究所达成科技合作协议,在燕麦、冬黑麦、荞麦、马铃薯、豌豆等作物良种选育、栽培和加工技术等领域开展合作,取得令中俄双方满意的合作成果。

中俄科学家合作育成的首个冬黑麦新品种"白BK01"的大面积推广,对中俄黑麦新产品研发、加工工艺创新、生态环境保护、特色产业升级、中俄贸易途径拓展产生了深远的影响。

(二)下一步工作

未来,双方将在以下几个方面进一步合作。

第一,特色农作物种质资源联合创新。俄罗斯幅员辽阔,地处高纬度地区,经度跨度大,生态环境复杂,农作物资源类型多样,多具有抗逆性强、稳产性好、品质优良的特点,很多特异基因是中国现有资源所不具备的。因此,有针对性地引进和利用不同类型的品种资源,与中国国内优异资源整合,做到引进、消化、吸收再创新,是中俄联合实验室的重点工作之一。

第二,特色农作物选育新品种联合创新。该项目将加强与相关国家科研机构的联系与交流,通过聘请专家和派出学习等方式,引进育种技术方法,结合中国特色农作物资源的优势和特点进行整合,利用体系的人才优势,针对中国国内多样化的自然生态条件,完善中国特色作物育种体系,以指导中国特色作物育种工作。

第三,特色农作物栽培技术集成创新。研究不同作物的生理特点,进行不同区域的适应性试验和基因—环境互作试验,结合中国的自然与生产条件,依据生产发展趋势研究适宜的栽培技术措施,针对特色农作物品种创新,切实开展配套栽培技术研究,具体内容包括栽培生理研究、种植模式研究、机械化生产技术等综合技术集成创新研究等。

三、合作特色

（一）合作效益

通过联合实验室的建立,充分利用国外燕麦优异资源,开展国际间科技合作,开展深层次科学研究,快速提高中国自主创新能力,努力解决中国吉林省西部地区农业产业发展的瓶颈问题,带动相关领域产业进步。

通过联合建设,探索国内外多角度、多领域的技术融合和产品联合开发,推进中国燕麦研究与开发的国际化进程,构建国际化的技术融合—试验示范—联合开发发展模式,为中国燕麦类跨越式发展提供技术支撑和人才支撑。

（二）合作空间

以重点突破、辐射全局的战略思维,集中资金、技术和人才优势,加强中俄双方在农业科研开发、农业生态保护与治理、有机农产品培育、先进农产品加工技术等多领域的广泛深入合作。

通过组建联合实验室,建立中俄科研成果示范基地,为中俄农业发展提供技术支撑和服务,带动"一带一路"沿线国家农业绿色可持续发展。

（三）示范效应

该项目的示范效应主要体现在以下几个方面。

一是可联合推动中俄农业科技创新能力整体提升。中俄特色农业国际联合实验室是在中俄农业广泛开展合作的基础上,结合相互已具有的农业科研优势和发展需求,有目的、有针对性地进行技术融合和科技资源共享,并共同开展实验,形成科技合力,必将推动相关领域创新能力的大幅度提升。

二是可带动中俄两国特色农业发展优势区形成和发展。国际联合实验室的建立是立足于两国相关区域有针对性地进行合作融合再创新,科研成果与农业发展实际有较高的契合度。必将支撑各自特色农业的发展,也必然会形成各自的农业发展优势区,带动农业综合生产能力的提高。

三是可拉动中俄农业产业合作与联合发展。中俄特色农业国际联合实验室的建立,研究方向将不仅仅是种植,而是要向产品研发方面延伸和拓展,相关的加工及产业化成果将通过转化,带动特色农业产业的进步,也将拉动双方企业共同参与,促进共同联合,形成以加工成果为纽带、联合生产基地为支撑、企业联合集群为动力、开发系列特色产品为目标的中俄特色农业经济联系体系。

案 例 十

俄罗斯犹太州北方公司农业种植项目

◇◇◇

一、合作概览

(一)总体情况

俄罗斯犹太州北方农业公司是 2013 年注册成立的中国独资公司,公司注册资本 3300 万卢布,出资人为勤得利农场宝隆渔业有限责任公司,注册地为比罗比詹市。

公司从俄罗斯下列区政府、比罗比詹区政府及其他俄罗斯农业公司租赁农业用地 20000 多公顷开展农业种植项目,公司已累计投资 6000 多万元人民币。

(二)合作价值

公司与日本、加拿大、澳大利亚、韩国、朝鲜等国家的粮食企业建立了长期稳定的合作关系,在联结多方合作中具有重要作用。

该项目与中国黑龙江省农科院联合在俄罗斯建立了科技试验示范基地,种植品种多样,如大豆、玉米、水稻、小麦、马铃薯、人参,能够借助产学研平台并充分利用当地资源开发新品种。

二、合作实施

(一)完成项目和进行中项目

俄罗斯犹太州北方农业公司是俄罗斯犹太州最大的中国独资农业企业,也是远东区域最大的独资种植企业,在俄罗斯犹太州已经连续六年持续经营,经济效益和社会效益收获颇丰。

目前,已投资修建了 15000 公顷土地的水利、道路及其配套设施,建有水泥涵管制造厂、烘干塔、水稻加工厂等,已开垦荒地 15000 公顷,并种植了大豆、水稻、玉米、小麦等农作物,年产粮食 4 万吨。

俄罗斯犹太州北方农业公司与中国黑龙江省农业科学院合作,建立了科技示范园区,试验种植了小麦、玉米、大豆、油用亚麻、牧草和绿肥等作物优良品种,2019 年公司又新引进人参种植项目,建立了人参种植种苗基地。

此外,公司已与日本北海道银行的综合株式会社签订了长期农产品采购合同,与澳大利亚 CBH 公司签署了战略合作协议,与朝鲜的月峰山会社实施了粮食贸易,与韩国农协建立了友好合作关系,并与加拿大经典农业股份有限公司签订了农产品销售合同。

（二）下一步工作

未来,企业将着重做好以下工作:将继续扩大种植规模,形成蔬菜种植、粮食作物种植、牧草种植及油料作物种植4个种植业板块;利用俄罗斯现有对养殖业的扶持政策,开展养殖业,实现粮食的增值;进行粮食仓储、加工、物流的一体化建设,利用俄罗斯农业产品成本低的优势,将产品打入国际粮食市场或返销中国国内。

三、合作特色

（一）合作效益

公司成立以来,严格按照俄罗斯国家的法律法规规范经营,公司拥有9名俄罗斯员工组成的精英管理团队,并从俄罗斯当地雇用工人100余人,极大地解决了当地就业问题;此外,公司拥有凯斯、约翰迪尔等大型农业机械100余台(套),已开垦荒地15000公顷,部分已通过国际有机食品产地认证,极大地推动了当地农业的发展。

（二）合作空间

未来,公司将与中国营口自贸区建立起紧密的合作关系,利用同江铁路大桥,建立一条俄罗斯至中国营口港的粮食通道,以低成本把俄罗斯远东粮食由营口港船运至中国国内各沿海城市的加工厂;与中国国内大型农业企业合作,在犹太州再打造出一个建三江农场。

（三）示范效应

对中国的中小农业企业起到示范指导作用,为计划进入俄罗斯远东从事农业的中国企业分享成功经验,避免走弯路;对周边的俄罗斯农场在栽培技术和农机使用上进行技术指导,提升了生产技术能力,多方能够借助优势共同合作;公司是当地政府对外宣传和展示的基地,吸引了日本、韩国、越南、加拿大、澳大利亚的农业公司多次前来参观考察,成为当地发展农业的典范。

贸易投资篇

案例十一

中蒙蛋鸡饲料和麸皮贸易合作项目

一、合作概览

（一）总体情况

中国内蒙古自治区包头市北辰饲料科技有限责任公司成立于2000年4月，是农业产业化国家重点龙头企业、国家高新技术企业、中国饲料工业协会理事单位、全国首批可溯源绿色食品试点企业和农业部饲料质量安全管理规范示范企业（见图11-1）。近年来，公司坚持走内外贸易相结合的发展道路，积极与蒙古国相关企业发展贸易往来。

目前，中方与蒙方开展的合作如下：与蒙古国乌兰巴托市AJIGANA有限责任公司开展蛋鸡饲料贸易业务；与蒙古国乌兰巴托市Tumen Shuvuut有限责任公司开展蛋鸡饲料贸易业务；通过中国其他国内企业开展从蒙古国进口麸皮贸易业务。

多方进出口贸易合作项目的开展,为中蒙双方企业合作共赢、互通有无作出了积极贡献。

（1）成品库房

（2）仓库库房

（3）机器人码垛

图 11-1　中国内蒙古自治区包头市北辰饲料科技有限责任公司内景

图片来源:项目中方执行单位。

（二）合作价值

蒙古国农牧业资源丰富,农产品生产潜力较大,但加工业发展较晚,技术相对较为落后;中国虽然在技术方面存在一定的优势,但是在资源方面存在一定的不足;通过将中国较为先进的加工技术和蒙古国丰富的农业资源相结合,对双方经济发展具有重要意义,双方发展潜力巨大。

二、合作实施

（一）完成项目和进行中项目

中国内蒙古自治区包头市北辰饲料科技有限责任公司与蒙古国乌兰巴托市 AJIGANA 有限责任公司、蒙古国乌兰巴托市 Tunen Shuvuut 有限责任公司签订贸易合作协议,从 2010 年开始连续向蒙古国出口蛋鸡饲料。

从 2010 年开始,中国内蒙古自治区包头市北辰饲料科技有限责任公司通过内蒙古自治区荣浩进出口贸易有限公司开始从蒙古国进口麸皮。

（二）下一步工作

中国内蒙古自治区包头市北辰饲料科技有限责任公司下一步的工作计划如下。

将进一步扩大与蒙古国的贸易规模,扩大蛋鸡饲料出口量,增加牛羊饲料出口,力争 3 年内饲料出口量达到 2 万吨,出口额达到 1000 万美元;将进一步扩大进口规模,在扩大麸皮进口量的同时,增加其他农产品进口,力争 3 年内年进口规模达到 1.2 万吨,进口额达到 300 万美元。

三、合作特色

（一）合作效益

从 2010 年到 2017 年，中国内蒙古自治区包头市北辰饲料科技有限责任公司向蒙古国乌兰巴托市 Tumen Shuvuut 有限责任公司出口蛋鸡饲料，年均出口蛋鸡饲料 6800 吨，出口额约 320 万美元，每吨饲料平均收益约 150 元人民币，年均收益 102 万元人民币，约 15 万美元。

从 2018 年开始至今，中国内蒙古自治区包头市北辰饲料科技有限责任公司与蒙古国乌兰巴托市 AJIGANA 有限公司合作，向蒙古国出口蛋鸡饲料，每年 7500 吨，出口额 350 万美元，每吨饲料平均收益 200 元，年均收益 150 万人民币，约 23 万美元。

从 2010 年开始至今，中国内蒙古自治区包头市北辰饲料科技有限责任公司从蒙古国进口麸皮，年均进口约 4000 吨，进口额约 80 万美元。进口麸皮每吨收益约 100 元人民币，4000 吨麸皮收益 40 万元人民币。

（二）合作空间

目前，中国内蒙古自治区包头市北辰饲料科技有限责任公司与蒙古国多家企业已经在蛋鸡饲料方面展开了良好的合作业务，并且经过九年多的合作，建立了稳定的合作关系。未来，多方在现有业务的基础上，继续加大业务往来，扩展贸易范围，进一步提升和增强多方之间的合作机制。

（三）示范效应

合作项目的推进有利于带动相关产业开展规模贸易经营,促进相关企业开展深度融合,实现互惠互利,为双方企业在农业领域的共同投资建设和稳定发展创造了良好的条件。

案例十二

中蒙饲料贸易项目

◆·

一、合作概览

（一）总体情况

中国辽宁禾丰牧业股份有限公司是国家级农业产业化重点龙头企业，是中国饲料工业协会、中国畜牧业协会副会长单位。

基于蒙古国地广人稀、冬季持续时间较长、畜牧业生产以自然放养为主、大规模和现代化生产短期内难以实现等基本特点，中国辽宁禾丰牧业股份有限公司于 2014 年开始向蒙古国出口蛋鸡饲料及饲料原料产品，并定期为客户提供技术服务，开展技术交流。

（二）合作价值

中国辽宁禾丰牧业股份有限公司在蒙古国按照牲畜类别并结合当

地的特点,设立标准化养殖小区,在养殖设备、饲养模式及饲料应用等方面进行科学化管理,对当地养殖户起到示范作用(见图 12-1)。

（1）厂房　　　　　　　　　　　　　（2）养鸡场

图 12-1　中国辽宁禾丰牧业股份有限公司的厂房和养鸡场

图片来源:项目中方执行单位。

可以为当地养殖户提供专业的技术服务和技术培训,通过专业知识的普及和宣传、开展经济效益分析等渠道引导养殖户接受饲喂模式的改变,可以提升蒙古国整体的养殖水平。

该项目的实施,将利于中国辽宁禾丰牧业股份有限公司在蒙古国市场业务的快速发展,并提高禾丰牧业在蒙古国的影响力及市场占有率。

二、合作实施

(一)完成项目和进行中项目

目前,中国辽宁禾丰牧业股份有限公司与蒙古国主要在以下几个

71

方面开展合作。

第一,以贸易业务带动直接投资,寻找蒙古国有实力的合作伙伴成立合资公司,从事饲料加工、畜禽养殖及屠宰加工等业务(见图12-2)。

图12-2 中国辽宁禾丰牧业股份有限公司蒙古国客户售卖的产品

图片来源:项目中方执行单位。

第二,将中国辽宁禾丰牧业股份有限公司先进的技术及管理经验应用于蒙古国市场的开发及项目管理,将科技成果转化为生产力,为客户提供培训和服务,以提升蒙古国畜牧业整体的发展水平。

第三,在当地培训及培养专职的技术服务人员,同时通过研讨会方式对客户进行培训,宣传先进的饲喂模式及饲养管理知识,促进蒙古国养殖观念的改变。

（二）下一步工作

未来,中国辽宁禾丰牧业股份有限公司希望能与当地有实力的、具有规模的养殖企业开展以下业务合作。

一是开展优质饲料的加工,引导蒙古国开展现代化的科学饲喂模式,帮助养殖户改变传统的养殖观念,逐步形成规模化养殖,提高养殖绩效,进而增加养殖户的经济收益。

二是利用中国辽宁禾丰牧业股份有限公司的海外投资经验以及专业的技术和管理优势,开展肉鸡产业化业务,包含养殖、孵化、屠宰和食品加工等环节。

三是开展蒙古国牛肉、羊肉的进口贸易业务。蒙古国牛羊存栏数量较大,且肉质鲜美,性价比较高,近两年已经有制熟的肉制品出口到中国,中国辽宁禾丰牧业股份有限公司将关注中蒙国两国关于蒙古肉制品贸易的相关政策,适时开展肉制品的贸易业务。

三、合作特色

（一）合作效益

虽然蒙古国牛羊养殖量很大,但处于初级的牧草饲养阶段;蛋鸡养殖较为成熟,并已经规模化;肉鸡和猪的养殖数量较少,未达到规模化,饲养水平和养殖绩效一般,但由于当地人喜欢鲜鸡肉及猪肉,因此畜禽产业化具有较大发展潜力。

由于蒙古国养殖水平落后,未能形成规模化,导致蒙古国的饲料工业及畜禽产业化程度低。蒙古国饲料厂数量少、规模小,加工工艺简单,多为养殖场配套使用,且饲料原料单一,大部分依赖进口,饲料成本高,技术配方能力低,因此,蒙古国总体的养殖绩效很低。

中国辽宁禾丰牧业股份有限公司发展目标是通过开展出口贸易,带动对蒙古国市场的投资,开发有潜力的客户资源,寻找有实力的合作伙伴,在饲料、养殖及屠宰加工等领域开展合作,在实现经济效益的同时,促进蒙古国畜牧业进一步发展。

(二)合作空间

项目的实施将促进中国辽宁禾丰牧业股份有限公司在蒙古国市场的业务发展,提高禾丰牧业在蒙古国的影响力及市场占有率,以实现较好的经济效益,同时促进蒙古国畜牧业的发展;扩大中国辽宁禾丰牧业股份有限公司在蒙古国市场的业务范围,除饲料领域外,还将拓展到饲料原料、养殖及屠宰等领域,进而提升禾丰牧业在蒙古国市场的经济效益;项目的实施可以起到示范作用,提高当地的饲料加工水平,带动养殖观念的改变,导入现代化的养殖方式,进而提高蒙古国畜牧业的整体发展水平;项目的实施,还将改善当地就业问题,增加更多的就业机会;通过规模化养殖、先进的管理及现代化的屠宰方式,进一步确保肉、蛋、奶等产品的质量及食品安全。

(三)示范效应

畜牧业是一个关乎国计民生的行业,也是一个朝阳产业,特别是对于蒙古国来说,更是经济支柱产业,同时具有极大的发展潜力和重大的发展意义。该项目的实施,将提升蒙古国整体的养殖观念,使其逐步进入科学养殖的饲养模式,提高肉、蛋、奶的产量,同时促进饲料工业的发展,促进畜禽产业化的快速发展。通过现代化的养殖方式及管理模式,规范蒙古国畜禽养殖关键环节的控制,如药物的管理及添加、疫苗的使用、卫生指标的监管等,可以有效解决蒙古国畜产品的食品安全问题。

案例十三

蒙韩国际协力机构合作项目

◇·◇

一、合作概览

韩国国际协力机构(KOICA)蒙古国办事处是 KOICA 的海外分支机构。

KOICA 成立于1991年,作为政府机构,KOICA 致力于通过实施韩国政府的赠款援助和技术合作项目,最大限度地发挥韩国对发展中国家的赠款援助项目的效益。

KOICA 将蒙古国选为"优先发展国家"后,对蒙古国的援助规模稳步增长。1991年至2011年期间,KOICA 蒙古国办事处提供了98.859亿美元的援助。

目前,KOICA 蒙古国办事处正在实施的四类援助项目包括:项目援助、培训项目、韩国世界之友项目以及与非政府组织的伙伴关系。这四类项目均以千年发展目标为基础,以确保有效实施。

二、合作实施

表 13-1 展示了蒙韩国际协力机构在农牧业领域的成功合作案例。

表 13-1 农牧业领域成功合作案例

项目名称	项目内容	预算
Khalkh gol 农业区农业和畜牧业项目	办公设施、190 平方米干草仓库、1950 平方米集约型牛肉仓库、525 平方米集约型牛奶厂 Zimmatic 品牌灌溉系统,用于牲畜饲料和植物育种的 155 公顷农田 用于种植地下植物的 3 个 70 米×5 米温室 13 公里内的基础设施建设 地下水井/钻孔 人力资源开发 设备供应	400 万美元
蒙古国国家中央兽医实验室改造项目	人力资源发展 设备供应	1300 万—1600 万美元

案例十四

吉蒙生态农牧产业国际合作园项目

❖❖

一、合作概览

（一）总体情况

中国吉林省吉蒙农牧产业发展有限公司成立于 2015 年 11 月 20 日，注册资金 1 亿元人民币，主要经营范围包括生态有机农业种植、绿色生态牧业养殖、农牧产品加工、进出口贸易等业务。

2016 年，中国吉林省吉蒙农牧产业发展有限公司在蒙古国苏赫巴特省图门曹克图县获得 2.5 万公顷农业用地土地使用权，建设用地 120 公顷，计划投资 12000 万美元建设"吉蒙生态农牧产业国际合作园项目"（见图 14-1、图 14-2）。

（二）合作价值

总体来看，"吉蒙生态农牧产业国际合作园项目"的实施在多方面

图 14-1　公司牧场牛群

图片来源:项目中方执行单位。

图 14-2　翻耕的土地

图片来源:项目中方执行单位。

产生价值,这主要表现在:

一是有利于技术的推广。园区的建设极大地推进了蒙古国绿色农业种植和无害牧业养殖技术的推广。

二是有利于环境的保护。园区内将开发绿色生态农业项目和传统绿色牧业项目,对当地自然环境和生态系统的保护具有重要作用。

三是有利于当地的就业。目前雇用当地牧民55人,通过"公司+牧民"这一模式,未来将带动蒙古国350户牧民共同致富。

四是有利于产业的融合。园区进一步开发和实施生态旅游项目,通过将休闲农业和生态旅游纳入传统的农牧业之中,进一步推动当地的经济发展。

二、合作实施

(一)完成项目和进行中项目

目前,该项目的部分前期工作已经完成,诸如投资建设、协议签订、土地流转、设施建设等多个方面,具体为:

已完成购买土地的资金支付4500万元。

已获得蒙古国、中国吉林省政府批示文件,已完成中国吉林省长春市经济技术开发区发改委备案、长春市发改委备案、吉林省发改委备案并向国家发改委提出申请备案。

已获得"吉蒙生态农牧产业国际合作园区"土地检测报告、气候检测报告,已签署蒙古国土地转让合同、获得土地证、营业执照、土地测绘图,公司、农户(牧民)合作意向已签字确认。

园区部分土地已完成翻耕、整平,已完成将近 20 种农产品试种(见图 14-3),已种植 6 万亩燕麦草,园区目前养牛 5000 头、羊 20000 只。

（1）丰收的燕麦草　　　　　　（2）甜菜试种园

图 14-3　园区种植的产品

图片来源:项目中方执行单位。

已办理完 120 公顷建设用地的审批手续,已发放土地使用证,已完成 120 公顷建设用地的围栏和临时办公生活场所的搭建。

(二)下一步工作

未来,该项目将重点做好以下事项。

一是进行招商和融资,即在现有基础设施建设的基础上,不断通过招商融资扩充项目内容,促进项目多样化发展;但目前存在融资难的问题,投资农业风险高、投资周期长、回报慢。

二是进一步完善和巩固园区基础设施建设,即在保护好当地生态环境的基础上,根据项目需求完善基础设施建设,为项目的后续发展提供坚实的基础保障。

三是做好市场调研,开展项目风险评估,为未来项目的具体实施和执行做好前期准备。

四是积极申请农产品回运国内的配额,尤其是本公司在境外生产的燕麦产品回运。

三、合作特色

(一)合作效益

该项目内容涉及对原生态农产品和畜牧产品进行生产加工,项目将创建以"克鲁伦河"为主题的园区产品商标品牌,一方面将促进当地农产品和畜牧产品加工业的发展,另一方面将资源产品回运国内,进一步丰富了国内农产品的供给。

此外,还涉及发展草原生态旅游,这不但从市场的角度保护了当地的生态环境,也为当地农牧业的综合发展提供了良好的示范。

(二)合作空间

蒙古国资源丰富,具备开展绿色生态农业优势,该项目将结合蒙古国的自然资源优势,利用蒙古国土地和水源无污染的天然条件开发绿色生态农业,具有较强的可持续性。

该项目通过"公司+牧民"的合作模式无偿向项目周边牧民提供牧场,通过发展传统绿色牧业,进一步促进该项目的良性循环发展。

(三)示范效应

该项目以生产加工为核心,以市场为导向,坚持绿化环保可持续发展的理念,能够为当地生态农牧产业链条的打造提供样板。

将第一产业种植业和畜牧业与第三产业休闲农业和生态旅游业相结合,创新了产业发展模式,通过产业链延伸,提升了农牧产品的价值,促进了当地农牧民增产增收。

打造绿色优质的产品品牌,在蒙古国建成具有国际水平的示范园区,借助中国"一带一路"倡议的实施,增强了两国之间在农牧业生产、贸易等多方面的合作,为中国其他企业在"一带一路"沿线上的合作提供了示范作用。

案例十五

中俄农产品分拨配送中心项目

•❖•

一、合作概览

（一）总体情况

2016 年,满洲里市德丰贸易有限责任公司在俄罗斯伊尔库茨克市注册成立刘姆肯尔私人有限公司,注册资金 35 万美元,投资 500 余万元建设跨境农产品分拨配送中心。

该项目有效推动了农产品跨境销售服务水平,增强了果蔬在俄罗斯远东地区的市场竞争力和影响力,深受当地消费者信赖和好评,促进菜农果农既增产又增收。

（二）合作价值

中国农产品产量丰富,品种齐全,果蔬大量出口俄罗斯。由于俄罗斯冬季寒冷而漫长,农产品市场存在较大缺口,尤其对果蔬需求量较大,冬季虽然运输便捷,但因储存不当造成果蔬类农产品冻害损失严重。

该项目投资跨境农产品储存分拨配送中心,可有效降低农产品出口因储存不当而造成的损失,同时也可降低劳动力成本。

二、合作实施

(一)完成项目

2016 年,中国内蒙古自治区满洲里市德丰贸易有限责任公司在俄罗斯伊尔库茨克市注册成立刘姆肯尔私人有限公司;目前已经投资 500 余万元建设跨境农产品分拨配送中心。

(二)进行中项目

中国内蒙古自治区满洲里市德丰贸易有限责任公司于 2018 年 6 月再投入资金 85.3 万元人民币;完成恒温保鲜库 304 平方米的主体工程和果蔬加工分拨配送处理中心 575 平方米的主体工程,轻钢屋架正在制作安装当中。

(三)下一步工作

加快项目建设进程,促进中国满洲里对俄出口贸易快速增长和健康持续发展,将中俄果蔬进出口加工行业推向新的高度,带动农口企业向着规模化、科学化、产业化方向发展。

三、合作特色

（一）合作效益

2018 年项目投入运营后年增加利润 180 万元,总成本费用年均 105 万元,新增利润总额 75 万元。目前农产品分拨配送处理中心年周转果蔬 5 万吨。

（二）合作空间

该项目将把加工生产和资源循环利用有机的结合起来,可增大满洲里地区双边贸易经济总量,从而推动中俄农业合作在该地区蓬勃发展。该项目建成将促进中俄双方在该区域内其他相关行业的发展,增加就业机会,增加当地群众的收入,对社会稳定、当地人民走向富裕、推动社会主义经济发展起到积极作用。

（三）示范效应

带动全国果蔬基地的发展,目前涉及的基地有 40 多个;可以充分发挥各地方资源优势,发展地方农业经济。该项目不仅具有良好的经济效益,同时还具有很好的社会效益,符合农业经济的可持续发展的要求;项目建设投入运营后能够与项目周边的产业、经济、人文、社会等环境的发展保持一致,与周围社会环境具有良好的相互适应性。

案例十六

中国禾丰牧业有限公司俄罗斯项目

◇◇◇◇◇◇◇◇◇◇◇◇◇◇◇◇◇◇◇◇◇◇◇◇◇◇◇◇◇◇◇◇◇

一、合作概览

（一）总体情况

中国辽宁禾丰牧业股份有限公司（以下简称"禾丰牧业"）是国家级农业产业化重点龙头企业，是中国饲料工业协会、中国畜牧业协会副会长单位。

2018年，禾丰牧业与俄罗斯伊瓦责任有限公司合资，成立俄罗斯禾丰牧业有限公司，公司位于滨海边疆区十月区波克罗夫卡边境城市，是离中国最近的境外园区，亦是黑龙江省对俄合作境外示范园区。

总规划面积4平方千米，已取得完备园区法律手续的土地面积3.6平方千米，建筑面积达到13.5万平方米。

（二）合作价值

俄罗斯作为"一带一路"沿线国家之一，是中国进行对外直接投资的重要对象，两国之间地理相邻、文化相通、资源互补，拥有巨大的投资潜力。

项目投资地点在俄罗斯滨海边疆区乌苏里斯克，该地区内成熟的饲料企业相对较少，大规模且养殖效益高的猪场、蛋鸡场并不多。俄罗斯禾丰牧业有限公司的战略规划是发展成饲料生产商，开展生猪养殖、蛋鸡养殖业务和饲料原料贸易业务，为当地百姓提供优质的猪肉产品和鸡蛋，造福社会；为周边养殖场和自营养殖场供给饲料产品（见图16-1），节约资源，保护环境，提高养殖经济效益。

二、合作实施

（一）完成项目和进行中项目

2018年，禾丰牧业与伊瓦责任有限公司合资，成立俄罗斯禾丰牧业有限公司，主要业务为饲料及饲料添加剂的生产和销售；粮食种植、收购及贸易；饲料原料销售；家禽、牲畜饲养；等等。

该项目总投资金额为2800万元人民币（按1∶6.82汇率折算，约合410.56万美元），其中，辽宁禾丰牧业股份有限公司投资1540万人民币（约合225.81万美元），占55%的股份；俄方以生物资产投资，投资总额1260万人民币（约合184.75万美元），占45%的股份。

目前，合资公司暂时租赁猪场和蛋鸡养殖场（见图16-2）及饲料厂（见图16-3），开展生猪和蛋鸡养殖及猪肉和鸡蛋的销售业务。

图 16-1　产品认证书

图片来源：项目中方执行单位。

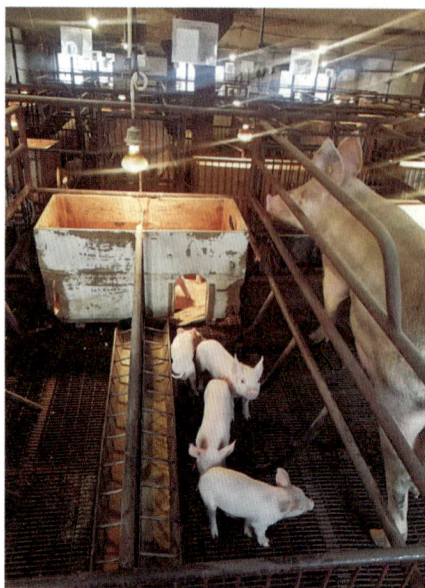 

（1）养猪场　　　　　　　　　　　　（2）蛋鸡养殖场

图16-2　俄罗斯禾丰牧业有限公司租凭的猪场和蛋鸡养殖场

图片来源:项目中方执行单位。

图16-3　饲料厂实验室

图片来源:项目中方执行单位。

（二）下一步工作

未来三年规划：新建预混料工厂，开展商业饲料的生产和销售；陆续改造及新建猪场和鸡场，扩大养殖规模，提高养殖效率。

三、合作特色

（一）合作效益

通过本项目的实施，可以改变当地的养殖模式，提高养殖户的经济效益；通过向社会供应优质的、安全放心的鸡蛋和猪肉，并保证食品安全，有助于实现农业产业的转型升级；该项目的建立，提高了禾丰牧业在俄罗斯的市场占有率和品牌影响力。禾丰牧业将凭借自身优势，为该项目在海外的发展提供良好的现代技术支撑，使其形成规模效益和品牌优势，最终发展成为生产技术设施优良、产品品质一流、生产经营理念先进、在俄罗斯饲料生产和畜牧养殖领域有重大影响力的现代化企业。

（二）合作空间

俄罗斯禾丰牧业有限公司借助禾丰牧业在中国国内的饲料配方技术、高效养殖饲喂技术等资源优势，未来在当地市场环境中，将以更低的料肉比、更低的死淘率、更高的产蛋率，促进养殖效益的提升。

（三）示范效应

俄罗斯禾丰牧业有限公司借助禾丰牧业在中国国内的饲料配方技术、高效养殖饲喂技术等资源优势,共享核心知识技术,在境外与外方开展了高效养殖模式。该项目的开展一方面能够充分发挥中方在合作中的技术优势,另一方面能够充分挖掘外方的市场优势,两者通过共同合作,实现双方企业互利共赢,共同推动了技术和市场的发展。

案例十七

中俄果蔬大棚种植技术推广与
果蔬保鲜库建设项目

◇◇◇◇◇◇◇◇◇◇◇◇◇◇◇◇◇◇◇◇◇◇◇◇◇◇◇◇◇◇◇◇◇◇

一、合作概览

（一）总体情况

中国辽宁省沈阳市威云果品有限公司成立于 2013 年，注册资金
500 万元，主要从事果品收购、储存、销售、加工（包装）业务，企业自成
立至今已连续多年荣获"辽宁省产业化龙头企业"称号，连续两届获得
沈阳市重点项目认证。

该公司在俄罗斯克拉斯诺亚尔库茨克建立优质经济作物种植示范
园区，并建立仓储恒温冷藏配送中心。此外，公司目前正在新西伯利亚
建设 1.5 万吨冷藏库建设项目，总储藏能力达到 15000 吨，占地面积
15000 平方米。

（二）合作价值

1. 有助于满足当地市场对农产品的需求

海外仓服务站本土站的建立和种植大棚技术的推广,可以有效减少订单的响应时间,提升物流配送时效,增加客户满意度,解决当地由于自然气候条件限制而导致的农产品供给不足的问题。

2. 可以极大地降低企业成本

境内农产品以及境外生产的农产品,运用当地的恒温冷藏库进行保管封存,可以有效降低物流成本,从而使得售价在当地果蔬销售市场处于领先地位。

二、合作实施

（一）完成项目

中国辽宁省沈阳市威云果品有限公司从 2017 年开始进行果蔬大棚种植技术推广项目,已经完成种子、化肥、农药等农资筹备工作,翻耙土地、播种、施肥和施药工作,田间管理工作,与俄罗斯科研机构和周边农户初步交流农业技术等工作。

该公司目前已经在俄罗斯克拉斯诺亚尔库茨建立起优质经济作物种植示范园区,投资金额 120 万元人民币,租赁土地 170 亩,建造了 15 个温室果蔬大棚,并建立了仓储恒温冷藏配送中心。

（二）进行中项目

目前,中国辽宁省沈阳市威云果品有限公司正在新西伯利亚建设1.5万吨冷藏库建设项目(见图17-1)。

图 17-1　建设中的冷藏库

图片来源:项目中方执行单位。

通过仓储物流建设,一是为海外仓提供配套服务;二是为国内外市场提供优质产品的仓储物流配送等服务。

该项目的建成将有效辐射于当地 X5 连锁超市(1800 多家)、马特米特(5000 多家)等大型连锁超市。

（三）下一步工作

在果蔬大棚种植技术推广方面,计划下一步扩大园区种植面积,预计最少种植西红柿 170 亩、黄瓜 130 亩等。

继续组织农业技术推广,加大示范推广力度,目标是在当地推广优质果蔬作物面积突破 500 亩,其中推广种植西红柿 300 亩,可增加种植收益 78 万元;推广种植黄瓜 200 亩,可增加种植收益 50 万元。

在果蔬保鲜库建设项目方面,完成现有建设项目施工,并逐步建成大规模仓储物流群及仓储配套设施,吸收更多的国外果蔬运营商、大型连锁商超等销售商达成长久的合作。

三、合作特色

(一)合作效益

1. 解决当地劳动力就业

俄罗斯果蔬保鲜库建设项目和果蔬大棚种植技术推广项目两个项目的实施,能够有效带动当地农业的发展,尤其是极大地解决了当地劳动力就业问题。

2. 显著提升当地农业产出

果蔬保鲜库项目的实施,能够解决当地农产品市场需求。以优质果蔬种植示范园区为依托,选育最适合俄罗斯克拉斯诺亚尔库茨克地区耕种的优质果蔬,培训周边俄罗斯农户耕作技术,推广国内优质种植技术,切实提升当地农户农业种植水平。该项目收获果蔬部分用于当地销售,优质果蔬力争运至其他俄罗斯联邦国家,为确保当地果蔬安全,建设境外果蔬储备基地贡献力量,努力实现经济效益和社会效益双丰收。

(二)合作空间

随着项目的逐步建设与完善,果蔬保鲜库建设项目建成指日可待。

项目建成后,可完善整个果蔬农产品国外市场产业链的建成工作,加快中俄贸易产量,实现中俄双边贸易共荣。

(三)示范效应

本项目具有两个方面的典型特点。

一是借助于境外资源优势以及境内资本和技术优势,通过在境外建立果蔬生产大棚并进行技术推广,有效地实现了优势互补。

二是不局限于传统的农业生产,而是充分借助于自身在农业生产技术和基地方面的优势,通过在境外发展仓储物流产业,不断拓展产业链条,实现现代农业发展。

案例十八

中国辽宁名优产品俄罗斯展示中心项目

◇◇

一、合作概览

（一）总体情况

中国辽宁沈阳俄中商贸有限公司成立于 2015 年 8 月 31 日，是一家专门从事对俄贸易的企业，并有旅游开发、经济信息咨询等资质。公司依托中国国内强大的企业资源及其在俄罗斯地区的强大号召力，与俄罗斯莫斯科市政府相关部门共同投资兴建中国辽宁名优产品俄罗斯展示中心项目。

该项目位于莫斯科市瓦勒尼斯娜亚大街"莫斯科国际食品城"，累计投资 180 万美元，海外仓占地 2 万平方米。展示中心以产品展示、体验、销售为主，结合 O2O 电商，致力于打造集仓储、展示、销售、物流于一体的一站式服务平台（见图 18-1）。目前已与多家俄罗斯知名品牌设备供应商和服务商建立了完备的电商运营以及销售团队。

(二)合作价值

可以加强两国优势产品、优良项目的互动交流,可以促进企业间的经济技术合作和文化交流,并帮助跨境电商提供完整的解决方案;为中国国内优质特色产品,尤其是中国辽宁优质产品"走出去"积极布局,作出了重要贡献,提高了出口产品的知名度,增强了国际知名度和国际竞争力。

(1)展厅　　　　　　　　　　　　(2)仓库

图 18-1　中国辽宁名优产品俄罗斯展示中心

图片来源:项目中方执行单位。

二、合作实施

(一)完成项目和进行中项目

项目于 2016 年筹划实施,地点位于莫斯科市新区国际食品城,莫斯科国际食品城,是目前欧洲最大的食品城,占地面积达 35 公顷,交通便利,品类齐全,客流量极大,而且客源遍布欧洲各地。

目前已经完成基础搭建,具备了产品展示销售功能。展示中心主要销售的产品为辽宁省内各种商品,如桦树茸产品、西红柿、彩椒、胡萝卜以及各色花卉。

(二)下一步工作

下一步工作的重点是做农产品的初加工、恒温储藏、冷冻仓储等项目,并计划投资脱水蔬菜的生产工艺及设备,以及生产桦树茸茶,并在俄罗斯、欧洲区域内销售;未来五年内,进一步强化和完善平台服务体系,个性化服务体验,致力于实现中俄物流集散中心功能,建立中俄欧盟销售物流中转中心。

三、合作特色

(一)合作效益

目前合资公司已经取得相关资质,同时逐步熟悉了俄罗斯法律法规、投资环境、市场需求信息等,建立了有效的国内外信息对接平台,为后期进一步合作奠定了良好基础;展示中心雇用莫斯科当地员工8人,未来随着合作项目的进一步加深,将对当地就业市场产生一定的带动作用。

(二)合作空间

该项目立足俄罗斯建立莫斯科海外仓,通过打造辐射欧洲国际营销网络、完善售后和物流服务体系,进一步扩大产品受众面、提升知名度。

(三)示范效应

该项目积极响应中国"一带一路"倡议,及时调整企业转型和优化结构,创新外贸发展模式,提高产品国际竞争力,为中俄两国在农产品贸易领域加强合作具有重要的推动作用。

案例十九

中俄农业生产基地建设项目

一、合作概览

（一）总体情况

中国黑龙江省绥芬河市宝国经贸有限责任公司（以下简称"宝国公司"）成立于 2000 年 9 月，注册资金 2000 万元人民币，是中国黑龙江省开展对俄农业合作十大企业之一。

近年来，宝国公司在俄罗斯建设了两个生产基地。宝国公司的整体运营框架：两个境外独资公司+一个境内粮食保税加工厂。境外两个独资公司分别是伊列娜有限责任公司和绿色田野有限责任公司。伊列娜有限责任公司注册地为俄罗斯滨海边疆区波格拉尼奇内区波格拉尼奇内镇；绿色田野有限责任公司注册地为俄罗斯滨海边疆区卡缅市。境内粮食加工厂为绥芬河市保达农牧产品加工有限公司，注册地为绥芬河市综合保税区（见图 19-1）。

图 19-1　宝国公司境内粮食保税加工厂全貌

图片来源:项目中方执行单位。

(二)合作价值

该项目充分利用境内外两个市场、两种资源,不断延伸对外农业合作产业链和发展空间。经过多年的发展,该项目已经形成跨境农业,并逐渐完成集境外种植、养殖、保税加工于一体的完整产业布局,能够在产业链的上下游之间相互衔接,一方面推动了俄罗斯远东地区农业产业的发展,另一方面也有效地解决了国内农产品供给问题。

二、合作实施

(一)完成项目

目前,该项目已经完成海外两个大型农业生产基地建设。

伊列娜有限责任公司在俄罗斯滨海边疆区波格拉尼奇镇内拥有可耕种土地8870公顷。绿色田野有限责任公司在俄罗斯滨海边疆区卡缅市拥有可耕种土地5220公顷。

上述两个境外农场拥有大型农机设备300余台(套),建有原粮烘干生产线、粮库、机械修理库、养猪场、化肥库、办公楼、职工宿舍等配套设施,生猪存栏6000多头(见图19-2),截至目前境外累计投资1.6亿元人民币。

图 19-2　在俄罗斯的养猪场

图片来源:项目中方执行单位。

此外,为进一步延伸跨境产业链条,实现境内外产业的良性互动,并充分利用保税区的保税、免税等优惠政策,绥芬河宝国公司在绥芬河市综合保税区注册成立了绥芬河市保达农牧产品加工有限公司,主要开展境外种植粮食回运保税加工业务,一期工程已投入9000余万元人民币,年产 10 万吨的玉米压片生产线已正式投产,年产 5 万吨的膨化大豆加工厂和年产 12 万吨的混合饲料加工厂建设也已基本完成,目前已进入试产阶段,全部投产后年可消耗大豆和原粮 20 万吨。

(二)进行中项目

目前,该项目正在有序开展中,并且取得了较好的成效。2017 年境外园区种植面积 1.2 万公顷,共收获原粮 5 万多吨;2018 年境外园区种植面积共计 1.4 万公顷,收获原粮近 6 万多吨(见图 19-3)。

图 19-3　在俄罗斯的种植基地

图片来源:项目中方执行单位。

(三)下一步工作

该项目将进一步扩大生产规模,延伸跨境产业链条,走现代化、生态化发展之路,2—3 年内实现在俄种植面积 2.5 万公顷(见图 19-4),

原粮产量突破 15 万吨,并完成绥芬河保税区加工区项目二期工程建设,形成集种植、养殖、仓储、物流、粮食深加工、畜牧产品深加工、高端品牌营销战略为一体的生态化、品牌化对俄农业合作企业。

(1)玉米   (2)大豆

图 19-4　宝国公司境外种植基地作物长势

图片来源:项目中方执行单位。

三、合作特色

(一)合作效益

该项目中的俄罗斯伊列娜有限责任公司和俄罗斯绿色田野有限责任公司两家企业极大地解决了当地就业问题,为当地农业的发展带来了活力。上述两家企业在俄罗斯共拥有员工 147 人,其中,中方员工 63 人、俄方员工 84 人。

(二)示范效应

该项目是典型的企业通过投资在境外建立农业生产基地进行农业

产业化发展的模式,通过投资创办企业,借助当地土地资源优势建立农业生产基地,有效降低了农业生产成本;此外,通过开展在保税区建立粮食生产加工企业,实现了产业链的进一步拓展。充分借助境内外优势,延伸农业产业链,形成集种植、养殖、仓储、物流、粮食深加工、畜牧产品深加工、高端品牌营销战略于一体的完整的农业产业体系布局,进而带动境内外农业产业的共同发展,这一模式对其他农业企业而言具有重要的借鉴意义。

案例二十

韩俄农业企业对话会项目

◆◆

一、概　述

目标:为韩俄农业企业间交流搭建平台;吸引农业领域的投资;加强合作。

举办周期/地点:每年一次,在俄罗斯远东和西南地区举办。

组织:主办方为韩国农村社区发展集团,协办方为韩俄两国农业部。

参会方:两国政府官员、农业企业主(涵盖小农场、农业设施、园艺和农业装备等行业)。

内容:介绍两国农业政策、推介两国农业企业;农企间召开会议。

预算:每年1亿韩元。

二、发展历程

2018年4月,在符拉迪沃斯托克举办首届韩国—俄罗斯农业企业对话会。来自两国的38家农业企业(含26家韩国企业和12家俄罗斯企业),就两国农业政策开展推介,交流信息,并举办企业间会议。

2018年6月,韩俄首脑峰会期间发表的联合声明指出,两国要定期举办农业企业对话会(以下为声明中的表述)。韩俄两国高度重视在农业领域的双边合作,双方同意定期举办两国间农业领域企业对话会。

2019年2月纳入"9桥战略规划"。建立企业家交流论坛,通过农业部门商业对话等对话渠道创造良好投资环境。

2019年6月,在莫斯科举办第2届韩国—俄罗斯农业企业对话会。来自两国的86家农企(含23家韩国企业和63家俄罗斯企业)举办企业洽谈会,推介业务(由韩国农村社区发展集团和韩国贸易投资促进局共同主持)。韩国北方经济合作总统委员会和两国农业部参会,韩方就"新北方政策"和农业领域合作政策开展推介活动。

三、主要成果

搭建了平台,促进了两国农企间务实合作和交流。为参会企业分别提供会议议程,协助参会企业探索新市场。

2019年6月,在莫斯科举办的第2届韩国—俄罗斯农业企业对话会的主要成果有:签订价值24.6万美元的两项作物加工设施采购合同;签署11项农业高科技合作的谅解备忘录,如智慧农场和无人机等。

案例二十一

中蒙博览会项目

一、合作概览

（一）总体情况

2014 年，中国国家主席习近平对蒙古国进行国事访问，把双边关系提升为"全面战略伙伴关系"。在此框架下，双方决定每两年共同举办一届中蒙博览会。第三届中蒙博览会于 2019 年 9 月 6 日至 10 日在内蒙古呼和浩特市、乌兰察布市和通辽市成功举办。

（二）合作价值

中蒙博览会是在"一带一路"倡议下组织的，是通过建立蒙古国—中国—俄罗斯经济走廊，推动东北亚区域合作的重要渠道。

二、合作实施

（一）完成项目和进行中项目

约有1200名来自蒙古国的嘉宾和代表参加此次博览会，共有450个蒙古国实体有机会销售其产品和促进其业务，这对于增加中蒙两国贸易往来、扩大互利合作具有重要意义。

（二）下一步工作

第四届中蒙博览会将于2021年举行。

Introduction

◇•

The Greater Tumen Initiative(GTI) is one of the most active intergovernmental cooperation mechanisms in Northeast Asia, mainly covering the whole territory of Jilin Province, Dandong City of Liaoning Province, Mudanjiang City of Heilongjiang Province, Hinggan League of Inner Mongolia Autonomous Region, the eastern provinces of Mongolia, some port cities of Republic of Korea, and parts of the Primorskiy Kray area of Russia. Thanks to geographical advantages, the cooperation among GTI member states have been deepened and remarkable achievements have been made in the agricultural sector. Take Jilin Province, China as an example, by 2018, more than 30 enterprises had engaged in agricultural development in Russia, of which more than 20 are in Primorskiy Kray, accounting for 80% of Jilin's investment in agricultural enterprises invested in Russia.

In addition to strengthening cooperation, cooperation among GTI member states in specific agricultural fields also becomes diversified, such as Sino-Russia Food Corridor Project, Sino-Russian Reliable Vegetable Basket Center Project, offshore fishery development and mariculture and other projects promoted by China's Liaoning and Russia. Different areas of the GTR have fully exerted geographical advantages, actively carried out agricultural cooperation and development, and made great achievements in economy, society and ecology through bilateral or multilateral cooperation.

1. The Major Modes of Agricultural Cooperation in the GTR

The major participants of agricultural cooperation in the GTR are mainly governments, scientific research institutes, enterprises, etc. Due to different cooperation purposes, different participants show different modes of cooperation in the process of agricultural cooperation. At present, there are mainly three types of cooperation modes in agricultural cooperation in the GTR.

1.1 Agricultural Cooperation Mode Characterized by Technical Research and Development

Focusing on the high-tech research and development of agriculture and guided by the cultivation of new varieties, joint research and development has been carried out in the development of germplasm resources, crop cultivation and breeding techniques, and improved crop varieties, which has greatly promoted the progress of agricultural science and technology, and laid a solid foundation for the high-quality development of regional agriculture. The main participants of the technology-oriented agricultural cooperation mode are usually research institutes. Governments further integrate agricultural enterprises into agricultural cooperation and R&D by setting up an industry-academia-research institute platform, which further enhanced the breadth and scope of agricultural cooperation.

In the practical process, according to different participants, the agricultural cooperation mode guided by agricultural science and technology research and development can be divided into two types.

The first type is featured by combination of governments and agricultural research institutes. This type is the main way to carry out agricultural S&T cooperation in the GTR. For example, the ROK government has signed an agricultural technical cooperation agreement with the Mongolian government, and the Mongolian University of Life Sciences has taken the lead in developing agricultural technology suitable for the Mongolian environment. At present, pilot projects have been completed for the breeding of improved forage crop(alfalfa), and the use of roughage and enhanced nutrition technology to improve the yield and genetic value of lambs and wools, agricultural scientific research, training and demonstration farms. The effect of cooperation is extremely remarkable. The Baicheng Academy of Agricultural Sciences of Jilin Province, China has carried out agricultural S&T cooperation with several Russian agricultural scientific research institutions headed by the Russian National Academy of Sciences to establish an international joint laboratory for agricultural products with Chinese and Russian characteristics, and promote technological breakthroughs and innovations in key areas such as the breeding of new varieties of featured crops in the two countries, the integration of high-efficient cultivation techniques, and the processing and utilization of featured agricultural products. The Inner Mongolia Academy of Agriculture and Animal Husbandry Sciences of China and Russia have established the "Inner Mongolia Sino-Russian Cooperation Center for Plant Technology Research". Through the implementation of Sino-Russian scientific and technological cooperation projects with Russian Vavilov Plant Genetic Resources Research Institute, Voronezh State University and other overseas units, new progress has been made in the cultivation of sugar beet, corn, Jerusalem artichoke, wheat, hemp and other crops.

The second type is the cooperative development mode with agricultural research institutes and enterprises as main participants, that is, agricultural scientific research institutes as the main body for R&D, enterprises as the main body for promoting scientific research achievements. They cooperate to promote agricultural S&T from research to practice. Among them, a typical case is the Agricultural and Animal Products Processing Center of China Inner Mongolia Academy of Agriculture and Animal Husbandry Sciences, which cooperated with the Right Middle Banner Special Animal Husbandry in the Hinggan League of Inner Mongolia, Mongolia Bornuur Eco Foods Company, etc., to carry out the project of "Building a Base for Planting, Testing and Promoting Cold-resistant Rice and Soybean", and has made good achievements.

1. 2　Agricultural Cooperation Mode Characterized by Cross-border Investment

The cooperation mode guided by cross-border investment mainly takes agricultural enterprises as the main body, and builds domestic and overseas cooperation platforms by means of overseas investment. With the help of resource advantages, market advantages, capital advantages, talent advantages and technological advantages in different regions, agricultural industry chain is extended to achieve the coordinated development of different participants. In practice, this mode presents three features.

Firstly, wide coverage of cross-border investment and development. For example, at two sessions of Korea-Russia Agribusiness Dialogue held since 2018, two contracts worth US $246, 000 for the procurement of crop processing facilities and 11 memorandums of understanding on agricultural high-tech cooperation have been signed, covering areas such as smart farms and drones. The fields invested and constructed by Liaoning China in the Russian Far East cover agricultural cultivation, product processing, fruit and vegetable storage and trade, animal husbandry breeding and fishing. Among the more than 20 enterprises engaged in agricultural development of Jilin Province in Russia's Primorskiy Kray, the industries involved are also rich, such as Jinda Overseas Agricultural Development Investment Co., Ltd. of Jilin Prounce, Yuyao Industrial(Shanghai)Co., Ltd., Yanbian Weifeng International Trade Co., Ltd. and Hunchun Huarui Senye Biological Engineerhg Co., Ltd. have planted soybeans, ginseng, edible fungi, and alfalfa in the Russian Far East.

Secondly, cross-border investment and development rely on resource complementarity of two parties. Investors and invested regions can make full use of resource and market advantages such as land, labor, capital, market and other resources to reduce the production costs of investors, and bring considerable economic and social benefits for the invested areas. For example, Defeng Trade Co., Ltd. from Manzhouli, Inner Mongolia Autonomous Region has invested more than 5 million yuan in building a cross-border agricultural product distribution center, which has effectively promoted the cross-border sales and service level of agricultural products, enhanced the market competitiveness and influence of fruits and vegetables in the Russian Far East, and increased both the production and income of vegetable farmers. Another example is that from Inner Mongolia of China Viction Cashmere Group has established a cashmere primary processing enterprise in Mongolia, and the production cost has been reduced.

Thirdly, the direction of cross-border investment and development has changed from traditional industries to new industries, and gradually realized industrial transformation and upgrading. Taking agriculture-related enterprises which are market-oriented as the leading units, on the basis of traditional planting and husbandry, comprehensive agricultural projects were developed overseas, in which agricultural production, processing, import and export trade were carried out, a complete chain of eco-agricultural industries was formed. Thus, the integration and development of agricultural industries have been realized. In 2016, the Jimeng Agriculture and Animal Husbandry Development Co., Ltd. of Jilin Province, China obtained use right of 25,000 hectares of agricultural land and 120 hectares of construction land in Caoketu County, Tumen, Sukhbaatar Aimag, Mongolia. It plans to invest USD 120 million for the construction of the Jimeng Ecological Agriculture and Animal Husbandry International Cooperation Zone, which will contribute to the all-round docking of the agricultural industry and greatly promote the development of local agricultural economy.

1.3 Agricultural Cooperation Mode Characterized by International Trade

The agricultural cooperation mode is guided by market demand, and led by international trade. The distinctive features and potential advantages of regional development are highlighted, then multi-functional development which is cross-regional and cross-industry is formed, and finally the joint collaborative development of agriculture in the GTR is realized.

Generally speaking, remarkable achievements have been made in agricultural development in the GTR in terms of international trade.

In general, the agricultural cooperation mode dominated by international trade can be divided into three types.

The first is the general trade mode, that is, commodity production places and distribution centers are in China, and domestic enterprises conduct international trade in agricultural products through long-term cooperation channels and trading partnerships with foreign parties. This trade mode is used by many enterprises currently. For example, Baotou Beichen Fodder from China Technology Co., Ltd. has carried out agricultural product import and export trade cooperation business with AJI-GANA Co., Ltd. and Tumen Shuvuut Co., Ltd. in Ulaanbaatar, Mongolia, and has made positive contributions to the win-win cooperation between the two sides. Since 2010, Baotou Beichen Fodder Techndagy Co., Ltd. from China has continuously exported laying hen feed to the AJIGANA Co., Ltd. and Tumen Shuvuut Co., Ltd. in Ulaanbaatar, Mongolia, with an average annual export volume of 7, 000 tons and an average annual export amount of USD 3. 3 million. In addition, the company began to import bran from Mongolia in 2010, with an average annual import of 4, 000 tons of bran and an average annual import trade amount of USD 800, 000.

The second is to build overseas trade platforms, that is, to continuously deepen the degree of cooperation with foreign parties by building a platform for overseas trade, and thereby expand its business scope. For example, the Defeng Trading Co., Ltd. in Manzhouli of Inner Mongolia Autonomous Region has carried out the construction of fruit and vegetable trading and warehousing logistics distribution centers with Russia. At present, the main project of the constant temperature fresh-keeping storehouse and the main project of the fruit and vegetable distribution and processing center have been completed. The service level of cross-border distribution and sales of agricultural products has been effectively improved, and the market competitiveness and influence of the company's agricultural products such as fruits and vegetables have been further enhanced in the Russian Far East.

The third type is an international trade mode based on the cooperation and division of labor in the industrial chain. That is, by adhering to the development path of combining domestic resources with overseas markets, the agriculture-related enterprises signed long-term cooperation agreements with overseas enterprises to realize cooperation and division of labor in the industrial chain. In the process of trade, cooperation has been carried out by making full use of their own resource advantages to further strengthen the stability of the two sides and achieve mutual benefit. China Inner Mongolia

Weixin Cashmere Group and Mongolian Hongju Co., Ltd., has reached an agreement in 2019 to acquire 500–1,000 tons of washed cashmere, with a total investment of about 450 million yuan, which will be completed by the end of 2020. According to the agreement, Viction Cashmere Group and Mongolian Hongju Co., Ltd. will start their work separately, in which the Mongolian side is responsible for the purchase, processing, inspection, quarantine, transportation and customs clearing procedure for export of the cashmere, while the Chinese side is responsible for raising funds, inspecting and receiving goods and other services.

2. The Main Practices of Agricultural Cooperation Participants in the GTR

The participants in the agricultural cooperation in the GTR are diverse, therefore, the practices of different participants are different. From a macro perspective, government departments are the guides to promote the agricultural cooperation in the GTR, and cooperation of trade, investment and S&T through plans and policies. From a micro perspective, scientific research institutions and enterprises are the backbones of promoting agricultural cooperation in the GTR.

2.1 Establishing a Scientific Research Platform and Boosting Regional Cooperation with S&T

The functions and advantages of different social divisions of labor(scientific research, education, production, etc.) in agricultural field are integrated to realize the docking and coupling of different links in agricultural technology innovation, thus promote the common development of agricultural technology in the GTR. From the current situation of the development of the regional agricultural industry-university-research platform, the main body of cooperation of the GTR is scientific research institute. In general, scientific research cooperation covers a wide range of areas. For example, the Inner Mongolia Academy of Agricultural and Animal Husbandry Sciences of China and the Animal Veterinary Medical College of Mongolian State University of Agriculture jointly launched the project of "Research on the Cooperation of Exploitation of Natural Veterinary Medicine Resources and Creation of New Drugs in Sino-Mongolia". The two sides jointly investigated and conducted collection and test of common natural medicines shared at the border. In addition, the two sides sent experts to guide each other's teams, and actively encouraged team members to exchange and communicate with each other, conducted long-term monitoring and timely feedback of the effectiveness of natural medicines, jointly wrote plan application materials, participated in experiments and data collation, and achieved resources and results sharing. The Baicheng Academy of Agricultural Sciences Jilin, China and Russia jointly launched the "International Joint Laboratory Project on Agriculture with Chinese and Russian Characteristics". It also cooperated with several scientific research institutions (such as the Russian National Academy of Sciences) in agricultural S&T, established the joint research platforms to promote technological breakthroughs and innovations in key agricultural fields of the two countries, jointly boosted the excellent germplasm innovation, technological integration and upgrading, and built the "advantageous producing areas of special miscellaneous grains and beans of China and Russia" and "distribution center of special agricultural products of China and Russia".

In addition, some enterprises have also participated in the construction of agricultural production, education and research platforms in GTR, and achieved good results. For example, in recent years, Jilin Academy of Agricultural Sciences of China has cooperated with the Far East Agricultural Science Center of Russian Academy of Agricultural Sciences, Jinda Overseas Agricultural Development and Investment Co., Ltd. of Jilm Prance and other agricultural units and scientific and technological enterprises, and carried out demonstration and promotion of soybeans, alfalfa and other crops of dairy processing technology in the Russian Far East and agricultural exchanges and cooperation. At the same time, the Sino-Russian "Far East Agricultural Science Research Center" was jointly set up to carry out the ecological experimental research on soybean, corn, wheat, alfalfa, potato and other crops. Among them, 100 hectares of Gongnong No. 1 alfalfa varieties were tested and demonstrated on the overseas farms of Jinda Overseas Agricultural Development and Investment Co., Ltd. of Jilin Proine, from which scientific research units and enterprises obtained good returns. The Temu Animal Husbandry Development Co., Ltd. in Inner Mongolia of China has actively participated in the research conducted by Inner Mongolia Academy of Agricultural and Animal Husbandry Sciences and Agricultural Research Institutions of Mongolia, and cooperated with many units to implement the "Sino-Mongolia Cold-Resistant Rice and Soybean

Planting Experiment Promotion Base Project". In 2016, a demonstration base of 100 hectares was built in Mongolia, and preliminary planting trials of three rice varieties and three soybean varieties in alpine regions were completed.

2.2 Establishing Overseas Production Bases to Realize Mutual Benefit

Based on the original business, agricultural enterprises built overseas agricultural production bases and obtained economic, social and ecological benefits by making use of complementary advantages of funds, technology, talents and resources at home and abroad. All of these provided impetus for the common development of agriculture at home and abroad. For example, Suifenhe Baoguo Economic and Trade Co., Ltd. in Heilongjiang Province is one of the top ten enterprises in Heilongjiang Province to carry out agricultural cooperation with Russia. The company makes full use of both domestic and overseas markets and resources to constantly extend the industrial chain. It has established two wholly-owned companies in Russia. After years of development, it has formed a complete cross-border agriculture industrial layout which integrates overseas planting, breeding, bonded processing as a whole. Russian Northern Agricultural Corporation is a wholly Chinese-owned company in Russia. The company has leased more than 20,000 hectares of agricultural land from local government of Russia and other Russian agricultural companies. The company cumulatively invested more than 60 million yuan in water conservancy and its supporting facilities, drying towers, land scales, etc. At present, 15,000 hectares of wasteland have been reclaimed and crops (soybean, rice, corn, wheat, etc.) have been planted, with an annual output of more than 40, 000 tons. The construction and implementation of the project has greatly promoted the development of the local agricultural industry, and it is of great significance to the long-term development of the local planting industry through wasteland reclama-tion and infrastructure construction. Besides, it further develops the primary processing industry of agricultural products on the basis of traditional plant-ing industry, continuously promotes and deepens the agricultural industry, promotes the development of industries such as warehousing and logistics, and realizes the coordinated promotion of regional economy as a whole.

2.3 Establishing Overseas Distribution Centers to Enrich the Local Product Market

Through the establishment of cold storage centers and distribution cen-ters abroad, agricultural enterprises have further connected the domestic production bases with overseas markets, realized the complementarity of re-gional resources and markets, and the synergy of supply and demand at home and abroad. For example, Shenyang Weiyun Fruit Co., Ltd., which is mainly engaged in fruit purchase, storage, sales and processing in Liaon-ing China, is currently building 20, 000-ton cold storage project in Russia Zabaykalsky Krai, covering an area of 20, 000 square meters. Through the construction of overseas warehousing and logistics centers, the local distri-bution in Russia of various fruits and vegetables from Liaoning China could be realized. The implementation of this project has further established the brand image of agricultural products of Liaoning China on the one hand. On the other hand, it has also solved the problem of insufficient local supply of agricultural products such as fruits in Russian border areas. Defeng Trading Co., Ltd. in Manzhouli City, Inner Mongolia of China, has invested more than 5 million yuan to build a distribution center for cross-border agricultural products. The implementation of the project has not only promoted the increase in production and income of vegetable farmers and fruit farmers, but also solved the problems such as the large gap in the agricultural product market due to the cold and long winter in Russia, and the serious loss of freezing damage to fruits and vegetables caused by improper storage. Shenyang Sino-Russia Trade Co., Ltd. of Liaoning China has established the "Chinese Famous and Excellent Commodity Exhibition Center" in Moscow International Food City. Its main products include birch antler products, tomatoes, color peppers, carrots and various flowers, which has enriched the local market.

3. Achievements of Agricultural Cooperation in the GTR

Since GTI was proposed, especially since the establishment of the Agricultural Commission in 2016, agricultural cooperation among member countries has been gradually strengthened, and the scope of cooperation has been gradually expanded. All parties have achieved mutual benefit in economy, society, ecology, etc. Overall, the achievements of agricultural cooperation in the GTR are reflected in the following aspects.

3.1 The Common Development of Regional Agriculture Has Been Achieved

The geographical scope of the GTR is relatively wide. There are also some differences among member countries in resources, systems, S&T, markets, etc. Regional agricultural cooperation will make up for the shortcomings among various parties to achieve the common development of regional agriculture. Taking Northeast China and the Russian Far East as an example, there are many similarities in agricultural production and crop cultivation between the two places. Russia is rich in land resources, small population and extensive cultivation. However, its scientific and technological support system in the optimization of agricultural planting structure has not been formed, nor has the advantages of local agricultural development and international competitiveness been upheld; China is weak in resource endowments, but it has certain guarantees in terms of funds. The cooperation between the two sides will inevitably form their respective agricultural development advantages, and improve the overall agricultural production capacity of the whole region. In addition, agricultural research institutions in China and Russia have carried out cooperative research and the research direction is not limited to planting. The relevant processing and industrialization results will, through transformation, promote the progress of the characteristic agricultural industry, stimulate the joint participation and cooperation of enterprises of both sides, and form a Sino-Russian agricultural economic linkage system joint production base as the support, the enterprise joint cluster as the driving force, and the development of a series of special products as the goal.

3.2 Great Achievements Have Been Made in Agricultural Technology

At present, agricultural technology cooperation among GTI member countries has made significant breakthroughs in some key areas. On the one hand, the problem of weak integration of agricultural product cultivation with the ecological characteristics in the region has been solved. On the other hand, the support system of agricultural technology has been further deepened. For example, since 2003, Baicheng Academy of Agricultural Sciences, Jilin Province of China has established extensive cooperation and exchanges with many agricultural academies in Russia. It has successively reached scientific cooperation agreements with the Northeast Regional Agricultural Research Institute of the Russian Academy of Sciences, the Samara Agricultural Research Institute, the All-Russian Cereal and Leguminous Crops Research Institute, the Tartar Agricultural Research Institute, the All-Russian Feed Research Institute, the Ural Agricultural Research Institute and the Irkutsk Agricultural Research Institute. Cooperation has been carried out in the breeding, cultivation and processing techniques of improved varieties of oats, winter rye, buckwheat, potatoes and peas, and satisfactory results have been achieved. The large-scale promotion of "White BK01", the first new winter rye variety, has been widely promoted by Chinese and Russian scientists. It has a profound impact on the R&D of new winter rye products, the innovation of processing technology, the protection of ecological environment, the upgrading of characteristic industries and the expansion of trade channels between China and Russia.

3.3   Regional Ecological Environment Has Been Improved

The cooperation among different parties in the GTR, especially the cooperation in the agricultural S&T research and development and promotion, has further improved the ecological environment in the region and laid a solid foundation for the healthy and sustainable development of the whole region. For example, the project of "Cooperative Research on the Exploration of Natural Veterinary Drug Resources and Creation of New Drugs in Sino-Mongolia" conducted by the Inner Mongolia Academy of Agricultural and Animal Husbandry Sciences of China and Mongolia enables the aquaculture industry to better meet the requirements of modern production and shed-feeding, effectively reduce the overload pressure of the grassland, and play a positive role in maintaining grassland, preventing desertification, conserving water, protecting ecological balance and sustainable development so as to achieve a win-win result of production and ecology. The project of "High-quality, High-yield and High-efficiency Planting Model and Technical Measures for Jerusalem Artichoke Planted on the Land of Sanhua (salinization, desertization and desertification)" plays an important role in controlling sandstorms caused by soil salinization, desertization and desertification. It is also of great significance in improving the ecological environment, promoting energy conservation and emission reduction, and realizing low-carbon economy.

3. 4 Regional Employment Problems Have Been Solved

Currently, the area of agricultural cooperation in the GTR is diversified, which brings vitality to the development of the agricultural economy in the investment region. At the same time, the agricultural cooperation among the GTI member countries, especially agricultural cooperation by means of overseas agricultural investment, has brought a large number of jobs to local area and solved employment problem. For example, the Illina Yiliena Co., Ltd. and the Green Field Co., Ltd., which are invested and founded by Suifenhe Baoguo Economic and Trade Co., Ltd. in Heilongjiang Province have a total of 147 employees, including 84 Russian employees. The "Jilin-Mongolia International Cooperation Park of Eco-agriculture and Animal Husbandry Industry", which was launched by Jilin-Mongolia Agricultural and Animal Husbandry Industry Development Co., Ltd. in Jilin Province, China, currently employs 55 local herdsmen, and will increase the income of 350 herdsmen after the completion of the project. The Northern Agricultural Company, founded by China in Russia, currently has a management team of 9 Russian employees with a wide range of expertise (legal, financial, tax, agricultural machinery technology, etc.). It also employs more than 100 local workers from Russia.

3. 5 Transformation and Upgrading Have Been Achieved in Agricultural Industry

The agricultural cooperation of all parties is not limited to traditional planting and aquaculture industries, but is further expanded on the basis of traditional industries, established production and processing bases in the field of agricultural products, upgrading and transforming the traditional agricultural industries, and constantly extending the agricultural industry chain so as to achieve mutual benefit for all parties. Liaoning Hefeng Animal Husbandry Co., Ltd. and its Russia partner jointly established the Russian Hefeng Animal Husbandry Co., Ltd. in Primorsky Krai, Russia. The total investment amount of the project is 28 million yuan of which, Liaoning Hefeng Animal Husbandry Co., Ltd. invested 15. 4 million yuan, accounting for 55% of the shares. Russia invested in biological assets with a total investment of 12. 6 million yuan, accounting for 45% of the shares. In addition to the traditional poultry and livestock breeding business, the project will also carry out the production, processing, sales, acquisition and trade of feed and feed additives to constantly promote industrial transformation and upgrading. The implementation of the project will promote greater profits, and create more jobs for China and Russia.

4. Future Prospects of Agricultural Cooperation in the GTR

The future agricultural cooperation should be based on the in-depth cooperation of agricultural S&T, constantly expand the agricultural industrial chain, promote enterprises of all parties to deepen agricultural cooperation, and vigorously promote agricultural trade ties, so as to achieve the common development of regional agriculture.

4.1 Jointly Plan to Write a New Chapter of Regional Agricultural Cooperation in the GTR

With the continuous advancement of the Belt and Road Initiative (BRI), the cooperation between China and neighboring countries is getting closer. At the same time, more and more countries have joined in this initiative, forming a new prospect of development. The GTR is an important area along the northern line of BRI. The well-being of the countries and regions along the BRI route has been continuously improved, and agricultural development is also advancing to higher quality. As an important part of regional cooperation, agriculture will play an important role in the common development of the member states of the region in the future. Therefore, in the future, member states should continue to consolidate mutually beneficial cooperation, deepen cooperation in the fields of agricultural S&T development, food security, trade in agricultural products, and agricultural and rural development, and jointly create an open and multi-tiered pattern of internal and external connectivity, writing a new chapter of regional agricultural cooperation in the GTR.

4.2 Jointly Contribute to the Progress of Regional Agricultural Cooperation in the GTR

The member states of the GTR are different in terms of resource endowment, economic development, and political environment. The demands of different countries in the process of agricultural development are also varied to a certain extent; however, as an inclusive, open and overall international cooperation mechanism, the cooperation among various parties will promote regional coordinated development. In the future agricultural cooperation, member countries should make full use of their advantages of regional agriculture, the markets and resources of all parties, adhere to the opening up of agricultural cooperation, and further expand the agricultural industrial chain on the basis of existing cooperation. We will deepen cooperation and development in the upstream, middle and downstream of the agricultural industry, and constantly strengthen bilateral and multilateral international exchanges and cooperation in agriculture so as to better serve the development of regional agriculture and rural economy. In addition, we should continue to value agricultural trade and use international trade to complement regional advantages. In view of the different markets in the region, we should continue to promote the organization and implementation of major agricultural produce fairs such as agricultural expo, and take this as an opportunity to build a platform for enterprises in the region. We should promote the continuous expansion of overseas markets for agricultural products with regional characteristics, improve the popularity of local agricultural products, broaden the import and export channels of agricultural products, and vigorously promote the healthy development of agricultural trade, so as to leverage regional advantages.

4. 3   Share Benefits to Break New Ground of Regional Agricultural Cooperation in the GTR

In the process of agricultural cooperation in the future, we should base on the in-depth cooperation of agricultural S&T, constantly expand the agricultural industrial chain, promote enterprises in GTR to deepen agricultural cooperation, and vigorously develop agricultural trade exchanges. We should continue to share the experiences and achievements of bilateral and multilateral agricultural cooperation in order to achieve the common development of agriculture in the GTR. In particular, in the field of agricultural S&T, member countries should further deepen the cooperation mechanism among various parties, share the fruits of agricultural cooperation, and use scientific and technological forces to promote the development of regional agriculture. We should continue to rely on scientific research institutes, innovative enterprises, and scientific and technological intermediary organizations to establish a service platform for agricultural technology exchange and cooperation, strengthen agricultural S&T exchanges and cooperation, deepen bilateral cooperation in the development and utilization of crop germplasm resources, crop cultivation and breeding techniques, and plant protection, promote a variety of models, such as the joint laboratory construction and demonstration base, and actively build a platform for production, learning and research. Besides, we also will promote the integration of production, learning and research, and the development of regional agriculture with the force of S&T.

Research and Development

Case 1

Sino-Mongolia Joint Research of Veterinary Natural Medicine Resources Development and Pharmaceutical Innovation Cooperation

◇•

1. Project Overview

1.1　Introduction

Since 2017, Veterinary Research Institute of Inner Mongolia Academy of Agricultural and Animal Husbandry Sciences(IMAAAHS) and College of Veterinary Medicine of Mongolian State University of Agriculture(MSUA) (See Figure 1-1) have worked together to carry out the project "Sino-Mongolia Joint Research of Veterinary Natural Medicine Resources Development and Pharmaceutical Innovation Cooperation".

Efforts have been made in the following aspects:

The two sides have combined the rich natural medicine resources in Inner Mongolia Autonomous Region with the large-scale cattle and sheep test bases in Mongolia. Researches on natural mineral medicines, such as rare earths, sodium humate, and key Mongolian medicinal materials have been carried out. The active components of natural medicines have been separated, extracted and purified. Pharmacological pharmacodynamics test, pharmacokinetics test and medicine safety test have been carried out. Quality standards have been established, and the production process has been improved. The innovation of Mongolian veterinary medicine has been developed.

The research results are promoted and applied to large pastures in China and Mongolia.

It exerts comprehensive pharmacological effects of antibacterial, anti-parasite, anti-inflammation and immunity. It publicizes the concept of green and healthy farming, train technical personnel and local farmers with rich professional knowledge, improves the prevention and control of animal diseases in China and Mongolia, and promotes the healthy and green development of animal husbandry.

1. 2　Significance

The cooperation between China and Mongolia in the field of veterinary natural medicines can solve the key problems in the prevention and control of animal diseases between them, and actively promote scientific and bilateral technological innovation cooperation, such as joint research projects

Figure 1-1   College of Veterinary Medicine of Mongolian State University of Agriculture

Source of the Photos: the Chinese side of the Cooperation Program.

and joint laboratories, and better facilitate the promotion of personnel exchange and training.

This project is designed to constantly deepen cooperation in scientific and technological innovation between China and Mongolia, increase the income of farmers and herdsmen, promote the healthy and green development of animal husbandry, increase the output value of agricultural economy, and contribute to the economic and social development of Mongolia.

2. Implementation

2.1   Completed Projects

Veterinary Research Institute of Inner Mongolia Academy of

Agricultural and Animal Husbandry Sciences (IMAAAHS) and College of Veterinary Medicine of Mongolian State University of Agriculture (MSUA) worked together to carry out the project "Sino-Mongolia Joint Research of Veterinary Natural Medicine Resources Development and Pharmaceutical Innovation Cooperation" and signed a cooperation agreement in 2017. after that, the two sides carried out field research on the test conditions, environment and animal test base. in November 2017, both sides joined hands to apply for China's National Key R&D Plan for 2018——the Key Intergovernmental Project for International Cooperation in Science, Technology and Innovation on "Sino-Mongolia Joint Research of Veterinary Natural Medicine Resources Development and Pharmaceutical Innovation Cooperation Project", which later was approved and funded by Chinese Ministry of Science and Technology.

Since the implementation of the project, both China and Mongolia have pooled their regional advantages, and the projects are progressing smoothly on schedule.

2.2   Ongoing Projects

It is a project that both China and Mongolia work together to collect traditional Mongolian veterinary prescriptions, and learn the traditional production technology of Mongolian veterinary medicine. At the same time, common natural veterinary medicine products, which have not yet been discovered, have been redeveloped and utilized to create a new type of green, healthy and efficient veterinary biological agents. It is the first attempt of both sides in this field.

Ongoing projects are as follows:

Screening 5-8 plant-derived natural medicines(stellera chamaejasme,
pomegranate skin, astragalus, spider, scutellaria baicalensis, artemisia an-
nua, red bean grass)and mineral natural-derived medicines(rare earths and
sodium humate). formulating new quality standards for veterinary medicines
and production technical regulations applicable to the two countries. com-
pleting the R&D of new products of Mongolian veterinary medicines. dem-
onstrating the application of new reagents for Mongolian veterinary
medicines in a number of cattle and sheep farms in Mongolia, so as to reduce the incidence of animal diseases and improve the utilization rate of
feed.

2.3   Future Plan

In the next step, the two sides will continue to complete the project
and the signed scientific research cooperation agreement, and strengthen
cooperation to consolidate the achieved outcomes.

3. Major Characteristics

3.1   Benefits of Cooperation

China and Mongolia have reached a common consensus in promoting
scientific and innovative cooperation under the Belt and Road Initiative. The
coordinating role of the intergovernmental committee on scientific and tech-

nological cooperation has been given full play. the cooperation has promoted scientific and technological cooperation such as join science and technology research projects, collaborative laboratory, technology transfer center in Mongolia. Innovative infrastructure, personnel exchanges and training, joint laboratories and co-finances research projects are promoted, which contribute to Mongolia's economic and social development, and the friendly relations between the two countries, and the cooperation in scientific and technological innovation between China and Mongolia.

Besides, this project can also promote the orderly development and utilization of natural resources, gradually change the mode of production of animal husbandry from the type of quantity expansion to the stage of quality efficiency, so that the aquaculture industry can better meet the requirements of modern production and grazing prohibition so as to effectively reduce the pressure of pasture overload, and play a constructive role in maintaining grassland, preventing desertification, conserving water, protecting ecological balance and sustainable development, thus achieving a win-win outcome in ecosystem.

3. 2　Fields of Cooperation

There is a wide-range field of cooperation of this project. The bilateral cooperation involves many aspects, which can be exemplified as follows (See Figure 1-2).

3. 3　Influence

This project will play an exemplary role for cooperation in other agri-

Case 1 Sino-Mongolia Joint Research of Veterinary Natural Medicine Resources Development and Pharmaceutical Innovation Cooperation

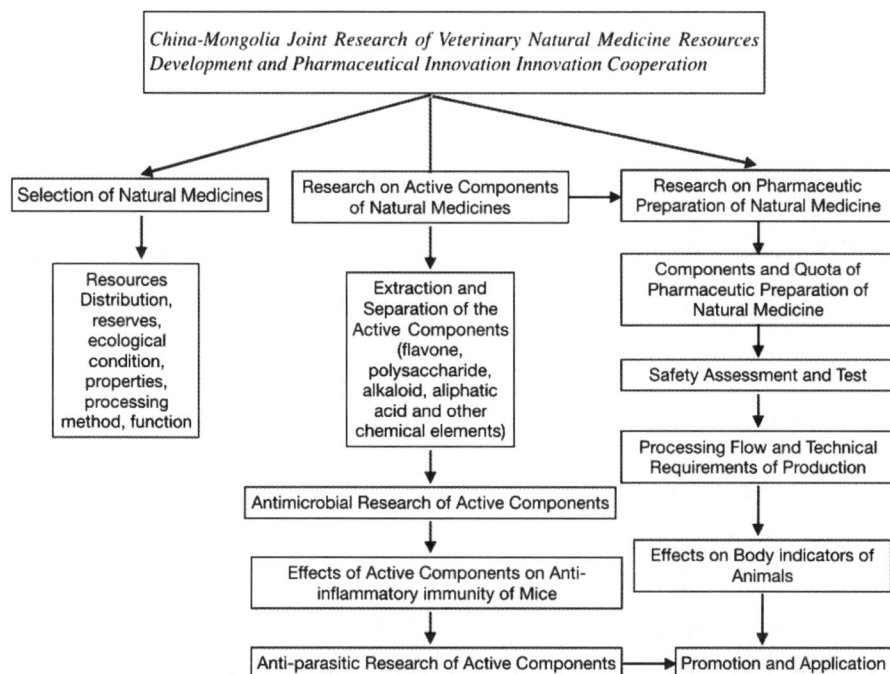

Figure 1-2 Sino-Mongolia Joint Research of Veterinary
natural medicine resources development and
pharmaceutical innovation cooperation

cultural sectors.

The project is innovative.

First, the proportion of natural medicine resources wide coverage is the first in China, which has good inhibitory and therapeutic effects on a variety of pathogens such as bacteria, virus, and parasite. Second, the medical research of poisonous weeds on pastures will bring about adverse effects. For instance, Chinese Stellera Root, one of the common poisonous weeds in Northern pasture, is increasing year by year. As a result, it formed dominant plant communities, leading to pasture degradation, hindering the production of animal husbandry.

The project is characterized by state-of-the-art research.

Based on modern pharmaceutical research, Veterinary Natural Medicine Resources Development of poisonous weeds can take full advantage of the medicinal value, restrain the spread of poisonous weeds to control pasture deterioration, protect ecological environment and make proper use of natural resources.In addition, the long-term clinical abuse of antibiotics has resulted in ever-serious side effects. Therefore, it is imperative to find an environmental-friendly substitute for antibiotics which can not only treat animal epidemics but also can reduce the number of drug-resistant strains.

Case 2

Agricultural Cooperation through
KOPIA Mongolia Center

◇•

1. Overview

1. 1   KOPIA Mongolia Center

Date of The Establishment: February 16, 2014 (the conclusion of the MOU between the Korean government and the Mongolian government: December 23, 2013).

Location: 4th floor, Research Institute of Animal Husbandry, Mongolian University of Life Sciences (MULS).

Objective: to carry out cooperative projects to develop and disseminate agricultural technology suitable for the Mongolian environment.

Target Area: 12 areas in 3 provinces including Tuv province (Ulaanbaatar), Selenge, Bulgan.

1. 2　Cooperative Institutions from Mongolia

Ministry of Food Agriculture Light Industry: National Agricultural Extension Center.

Ministry of Education Culture Science and Sport: Institute of Plant Agriculture and Science, Mongolian University of Life Science, Research Institute of Animal Husbandry

2. Progress(2014—)

2. 1　Progress: completion 5, under progress 5. The specific project development situation is shown in the figure 2-1.

2. 2　Completed project: 5 projects, total investment $ 592k from 2014 to 2018(See Table 2-1).

Table 2-1　Projects completed

Title of projects	Duration
Pilot project for propagation of elite wheat varieties and raising new cultivars	2014—2017
Pilot project for propagation of elite seed varieties of the forage crop(alfalfa)	2014—2017
Improvement in productivity and genetic value of lamb and wool with roughage and enhanced nutrition	2014—2017
Establishment of a model farm for agricultural research, training and production	2015—2018
Educational programs for farmers and agricultural extension officers	2015—2017

a. Elite seed Darkhan 166,144	b. Elite seed Darkhan−131, 34	c. Published materials
d. Open field, raising alfalfa	e. News release	f. Onion varieties
g. Farms in Belkh	h. Greenhouse inside of farms participated in the winter	i. Harvested corns
j. Potato seeding	k. Selection of cattle for testing purposes	l. Feeding forage

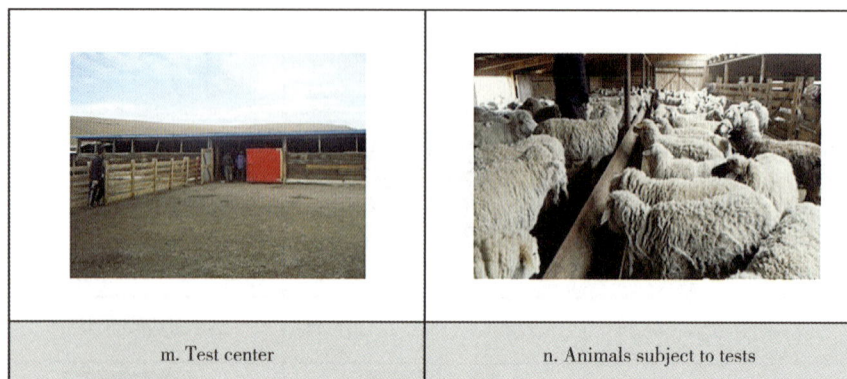

| m. Test center | n. Animals subject to tests |

Figure 2-1　Petails of the project

2.3　Under progress: 5 projects, tatal investment $ 190k in 2019 (See Table 2-2).

Table 2-2　Projects under progress

Title of projects	Duration
(Development) selection and distribution of Korean onion varieties adjusting to the Mongolian environment	2018—2020
(Development) selection and dissemination of Korean tomato varieties adjusting to the Mongolian environment	2018—2020
(Development) Application of customized specification technology to enhance productivity of Mongolian beef cattle	2018—2020
(Development) Project for propagation and distribution of seeds of perennial forage crop cultivars adapted to the Mongolian environment	2019—2022
(Demonstration) Pilot project for propagation of elite Mongolian wheat varieties and production of Mongolian registered cultivars	2017—2019

3. Major Achievements and Characteristics

3. 1   Project for Enhancing Crop Productivity

Propagation and distribution of improved wheat cultivars. The yield of 4 registered varieties suitable for the Mongolian environment amounts to 287 tons, which is equivalent to 38. 8% increase in productivity; and plans to produce 2, 000 tons of registered seeds in 2019.

Dissemination of technology for field experience and technology. Dissemination of technology, aiming to establish a pilot farm for vegetable cultivation under structure and to build a model farm or agricultural research, training and production.

Verification of Korean vegetables to confirm whether they adjust to Mongolian environment. Involving 5 cultivars of cherry tomato, 5 varieties of onion, 8 crops such as Chinese cabbage, lettuce, radish. Dissemination of technology for raising of seedling(grafting technology) and irrigation technology, improvement in soil fertility.

3. 2   The Improvement of Productivity of Animal Husbandry

Improvement in specification technology to enhance genetic value. Rotational grazing system, 3 feeding methods in winter; development of 30ha grassland for rotation grazing, with the profit increase of 290, 000 ₮/beef cattle. Increases in lamb and wool productivity by providing the artificial fertilization technology.

4. Existing Problems

First, lack of optimized techniques for the cultivation of vegetables and forage crops suitable for Mongolian environment. Lack of cultivation techniques for selected cultivars which can be grown in Mongolia(cherry tomatoes, onions). In need of the improved systemization of sustainable forage feeding programs.

Second, lack of professional professionals and agricultural educational materials suitable for Mongolian environment.

5. Plans for future progress

5.1   To Improve Technology and Agricultural Productivity to Adapt to Mongolian Environment

Systemic technology should be adopted to cultivate crops grown in environmentally controllable facilities and conduct tests in farms(Conduct tests in 5 cherry tomato farms, 2 onion farms).Produce 100 tons of fine wheat cultivars, 10% – 15% increases in vegetable output. Setting reasonable forage feeding standards to stabilize livestock management in winter.

5. 2   To Strengthen Exchange and Education of Agricultural Technology

To issue 2 reports on agricultural technology and carry out 3 education projects for farmers(90 people). Carry out a professional training program for Mongolian researchers：to train 4 forage feeding experts. Rural Development Adminstration(RDA) of Korea. sends experts to provide on-site consultation from 6 experts in onion, wheat, soil management, feeding.

6. Details

From 2014 to 2018, it has trained 3144 people through different training programs(See Table 2-3).

Table 2-3   Project training number statistics table

Number of trainees ＼ Year	2014	2015	2016	2017	2018	Total
Training at RDA	5	25	–	–	7	37
Expert invitation	2	18	1	3	6	30
Global training programme	4	5	5	5	5	24
Farming education for farmers	–	642	770	1, 233	408	3, 053
Total	–	–	–	–	–	3,144

Main Activities

(Source of the Photos：the Korean side of the Cooperation Program)

Case 3

Sino-Russia Demonstration and Promotion of Soybean & Medicago Sativa Varieties and Dairy Processing Technology Cooperation

⋄•

1. Project Overview

1. 1   Introduction

In recent years, Jilin Academy of Agricultural Sciences of China has cooperated with Russian agricultural institutions and Chinese tech companies to carry out agricultural exchanges and cooperation in the demonstration and promotion of soybean and Medicago sativa, and dairy processing technology in the Russian Far East. The institutions and enterprises that carry out cooperation include: Science Center of The Russian

Far Eastern Academy of Agricultural Sciences, Russian Coastal Agricultural Research Institute, Russian Far Eastern Agricultural Research Institute, Russian Coastal Agriculture Corporation, China Jilin Jinda Overseas Agricultural Development and Investment Corporation and its subsidiary Russia Saturn Corporation.

In addition, China and Russia have jointly established the Sino-Russian Far East Agricultural Science Research Center, which has carried out experimental research on the ecology of crops such as soybean, corn, wheat, alfalfa and potato, well as the collection and arrangement of lactic acid bacteria resources and the establishment of cross-regional lactic acid bacteria resources and other work.

1. 2　Significance

The implementation of this project will promote Russia to become an important base for exporting food and meat products to China and Asian countries. The project will also provide great potential for China's Jilin Province to develop agriculture and aquaculture in the Russian Far East.

Cooperation is carried out in accordance with the principle of "agricultural development technology first, experiment heralding pilot testing, and then popularization", giving full play to the advantages of animal and plant variety breeding, cultivation, agricultural machinery technology, animal husbandry and processing of agricultural products of Jilin Academy of Agricultural Sciences of China. At the same time, since enterprises and investment companies have funds but lack technology, this project provides strong agricultural technical support for many agricultural enterprises to carry out foreign cooperation.

2. Implementation

2. 1 Completed and Ongoing Projects

At present, cooperation has been jointly carried out in the following areas.

2. 1. 1 Screening, trial planting and popularization of high-quality soybean varieties in the Russian Far East

The Jilin Academy of Agricultural Sciences of China has cooperated with Jinda Overseas Agricultural Development and Investment Co., Ltd. of Jilin province to screen six excellent soybean varieties(Jiyu 202, Jiyu 204, etc.)Extension trials have been carried out on the farm of Jinda Overseas Agricultural Development and Investment Co., Ltd. of jilin Province(a subsidiary of Russian Saturn). The six selected varieties are suitable for planting and popularizing in the Russian Far East.

2. 1. 2 Screening, planting and promotion of alfalfa varieties in the Russian Far East

In 2018, The Jilin Academy of Agricultural Sciences of China, Russian Far Eastern Academy of Agricultural Sciences and Jinda Overseas Agricultural Development and Investement Co., Ltd. of Jilin Province(a subsidiary of Russian Saturn)signed a contract for the comparative experiment of alfalfa varieties and formulated a scheme for the comparative experiment of alfalfa varieties. Three alfalfa were selected varieties from each side, with a total of six varieties.

2. 1. 3   Demonstration, promotion and product development of processing technology of probiotics and fermented dairy products

The two sides jointly carried out the collection and collation of lactic acid bacteria resources in Northeast China and the Russian Far East and the establishment of a cross-regional lactic acid bacteria resource database.

More than 260 pieces of traditional fermented dairy products, sour cucumber and other fermented fruit and vegetable products were collected in the Russian Far East. By isolation and identification of lactic acid bacteria in our laboratory, 390 new strains of lactic acid bacteria were isolated from samples, including 320 strains of Lactobacillus and 70 strains of Lactococcus, which were numbered and preserved, and the fermentation characteristics and probiotic characteristics of the strains were studied.

In addition, the demonstration, promotion and application of probiotic processing and preparation technology in the Russian Far East were carried out, and a series of probiotic fermented dairy products, such as yoghurt, cheese and other new products were developed(See Figure 3-1).

2. 1. 4   The establishment of Sino-Russia Agricultural Science Research Center in the Far East Region

The Agricultural Science Research Center, jointly established by the Academy of Agricultural Sciences of Jilin Province of China and the Far East Agricultural Research Institute of Russia, officially signed the cooperation agreement and hosted the unveiling ceremony on November 1st, 2018

a. Bacteria Resources Preservation

b. New Probiotic Yoghurt Products

c. New Cheddar Cheese Products

Figure 3-1 Probiotic and fermented dairy products produced by the project

(Source of the Photos: the Chinese side of the Cooperation Program)

in Khabarovsk, Russia. The two sides aimed to carry out experiments on the introduction of soybean, alfalfa and cereal crops, as well as technical exchanges in animal husbandry and the processing of agricultural products.

2.2 Future Plan

The cooperation between the Jilin Academy of Agricultural Sciences and the Russian Far East in the above four aspects is being carried out as scheduled. On the basis of the Sino-Russia Far Eastern Agricultural Science Research Center, China and Russia continue to focus on joint studies on the

first three projects mentioned above. In the future development, the two
sides devote to making breakthroughs in technological research and development in the above three areas.

3. Major Characteristics

3.1   Benefits of Cooperation

Through cooperation, China and Russia have achieved economic,
social and ecological benefits.

In terms of economic benefits, the Jilin Academy of Agricultural Sciences of China has cooperated with Jinda Overseas Agricultural
Development and Investment Co., Ltd. of Jilin Province (a subsidiary of
Russian Saturn) to select a total of six fine soybean varieties, and promoted
planting area of 2, 400 ha in the Russian Far East with the soybean sales
income of 21 million yuan. The pilot planting of cold-resistant and high-
yield alfalfa varieties in the Far East of Russia was completed, including
36.7 ha of spring sowing with an achievement of 7.5t per ha in the first
year, with the sales income of 660, 000 yuan.

In terms of social benefits, 260 lactic acid bacteria strains were collected for the Russian Far East, and 390 new strains of lactic acid bacteria
were separated and identified, and the processing technology of lactic acid
bacteria and fermented dairy products has been completed. The Regional
Agricultural Research Center——the Agricultural Research Center of the

Russian Far East Agricultural Research Institute of the Jilin Academy of Agricultural Sciences of China was established with one joint laboratory was co-established to promote the exchange and cultivation of scientific and technological talents for agricultural cooperation.

In terms of ecological benefits, alfalfa is planted on hillside wasteland, and can grow and harvest continuously for 6 – 8 years once planted. The roots of alfalfa can protect soil and water, enhance the ability of surface vegetation coverage and effectively prevent soil erosion and control of land desertification. Therefore, this project will play a significant role in improving the ecological environment.

3. 2 Fields of Cooperation

At present the International Conference on Far East Agro-Industrial Complex: Scientific Achievements, held in Ussurik, Russia, in September of 2018, the Jilin Academy of Agricultural Sciences of China has made special reports on "Research Progress of Forage Breeding of Jilin Academy of Agricultural Sciences of China", "Research Progress of Soybean Genetics and Breeding of Jilin Academy of Agricultural Sciences of China", "Current Situation and Prospect of Biological Control in Jilin Province of China" and other reports. The two sides have further implemented the signed cooperation agreement, conducted comparative tests and demonstrations of alfalfa of the Far East Coastal Agricultural Research Institute and Jinda Overseas Agricultural Development and Investment Co., Ltd. of Jilin Province. Agreements on the experimental data collection, research, crop plant protection, technology exchange and other aspects have been reached.

158

3. 3   Influence

The development of this project is representative, of which the most important demonstration effect is the construction of industry-academia-research institute cooperation platform. Through cooperation with foreign scientific research institutions, scientific research institutions rely on agricultural enterprises established by domestic institutions in foreign countries, and have effectively established a scientific research platform for industry-academia-research institute cooperation, and gradually promoted agricultural scientific research and development. It has also continuously carried out the test and promotion of agricultural products. The construction of the industry-academia-research institute platform has effectively realized the combination of scientific research with the market, which on the one hand, gives full play to the enthusiasm of agricultural scientific research institutions in the process of joint cooperation; on the other hand, it has further strengthened the coordinated development of the agricultural markets.

Case 4

Training Course on Biogas Technology,
Rural Energy and Environmental Protection
between China and Mongolia

◇•

1. Cooperation Overview

From June 28 to August 16, 2019, Biogas Institute of Ministry of Agriculture and Rural Affairs (BIOMA) held a 45 – day training course on
"Biogas Technology, Rural Energy and Environmental Protection".

The training was held in Chengdu. 24 representatives from more than a
dozen developing countries, including Mongolia, Ethiopia, Afghanistan,
Mexico, Samoa, Libya, South Sudan, Ghana, Antigua and Guinea, participated in the training to learn biogas technology.

Among them, there are four representatives from Mongolia, including experts from Mongolian Commodity Exchange's Strategy Department, Province Intermediate Area Pasture Use Administration, Mongolian General Agency for Veterinary Inspection's National Food Safety Reference, Social Security Inspection Agency's State Inspector of Hygiene and Hygiene Control at the Department of Health.

2. Cooperative Implementation

This training mainly includes three main contents.

2.1   Classroom training

Classroom training includes 126 class hours of theoretical courses, 21 rounds in total.

The theory course is taught by experienced professors, and imparts professional knowledge, such as the development of biogas technology, biogas fermentation microbiology, waste utilization, biogas production and fermentation in large and medium-sized enterprises, new building materials and new biogas technology, introduction of digestion technology in dry air environment, etc.

2.2   Laboratory training

The laboratory training is divided into two parts: microorganism laboratory and central engineering laboratory.

The laboratory training lasts for 6 days (36 hours), mainly for research and analysis, including silica gel chromatography, microbial diversity, 16-year amino acids in the atmosphere, air-free environment of methane bacteria culture, TS / VS experiment of biogas fermentation raw materials, simple analysis of methane composition in biogas, etc.

2.3　Technical and practical training

The bioreactor construction company participated in the 5-day construction training; chengdu Amico Gas Power Co., Ltd. participated in Rongzhou's biogas detection project; chengdu Shunmei International Trading Co., Ltd. and Deyang Biogas jointly introduced the project of using biogas to clean chicken farm(See Figure 20-1).

a. Solution for local drainage system

b. Munkhnasan participated in the construction of bioreactor

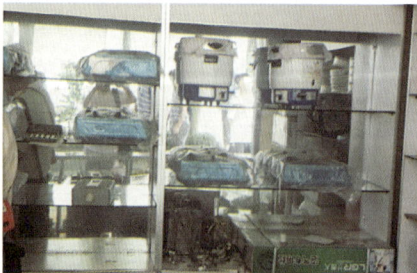

c. Household appliances using biogas

d. Local energy

Figure 20-1　Technical and pratical training scenarios

3. Benefits of Cooperation

Four participants from Mongolia participated in training courses on biogas technology, rural energy and environmental protection in developing countries and successfully completed their courses.

Mongolia does not yet have the capacity to develop technologies for rural energy and related environmental protection. This training will help Mongolia make full use of local energy, agricultural waste, electricity and water supply as well as non-chemical fertilizer to implement biogas technology.

Case 5

Agro-technological Cooperation
between China and Korea

◇•

1. Project Overview

Period and Budget:1995-Present, USD 1. 29 million.

Targeted Region:People's Republic of China.

Implementing Agency: (Korea) Rural Development Administration,
(China)Chinese Academy of Agricultural Science.

2. The Course of Cooperation

MOU on agro-tech cooperation between the RDA and the CAAS was
reached(April 9, 1994). To conduct joint research in areas of mutual con-

cern.

RDA officials were dispatched to the CAAS(April 19, 2001).

Joint Research Laboratory in the CAAS was established(December 11, 2015).

3. Major Achievements

3. 1　Agro-tech cooperation projects and exchanges

3. 1. 1　Joint research and expert exchange(1995-Present)

Joint research:a total of 89 areas, covering crop cultivation, breeding, and genetic resources, etc. Expert exchanges through joint research and exchange programs:700 researchers.

3. 1. 2　Establishment of Joint Research Laboratory, and dispatch of Korean researchers to China

Cooperation projects are explored to promote communication between the two sides, data collection and analysis on Chinese agro-tech; nine researchers have been dispatched since 2001;the 9th group of researchers has been dispatched(period:April 2018-February 2020).

3. 2　Sharing of academic achievements and information

Agro-tech Cooperation Strategy Forum has been held(1995-Present): 22 times

The sharing of academic achievement and new project exploration;

Consultations to promote cooperative relations and project development.

Symposium on the Internationalization Strategy for Medicinal Crops has been held(2015–Present) :4 times.

Joint efforts have been made to promote international standardization of medicinal crops and strengthen cooperation.

3. 3   Major achievements

In cooperation with the Institute of Special Animal and Plant Sciences (ISAPS) , the international standard of "ISO 19824:2017:Traditional Chinese Medicine——Schisandra chinensis (Turcz.) Baill: Seeds and Seedlings" was formulated for the first time in the world. It laid the foundation for promoting the international trade of schisandra seeds and seedlings.

4. Future Plan

The 23rd Agro-tech Cooperation Strategy Forum will be held on 2020, Jeonju, Korea. To share the achievements of cooperation projects, explore new projects opportunities, and have consultations to promote bilateral cooperation.

Case 6

Sino-Mongolia Pilot Demonstration and
Promotion Project of Cold-hardy
Rice and Soybean Planting

◇•◇

1. Project Overview

1.1　Introduction

In 2015, Horqin Right Middle Banner Temu Animal Husbandry Development Co., Ltd. in Hinggan League, Inner Mongolia Autonomous Region, China established partnership with Bornuur Eco Foods Trade (Tuv Province, Mongolia) and Fertile Soil Co., Ltd. (Orkhon Province, Mongolia) to jointly launch the Sino-Mongolia Pilot Demonstration and Promotion Project of Cold-hardy Rice and Soybean Planting (See Figure 6-1).

Horqin Right Middle Banner Temu Animal Husbandry Development Co., Ltd. hosts the project, and Bornuur Eco Foods Tradeand Fertile Soil Co., Ltd. participate in it by providing land and support facilities.

a. Rice Planting   b. Soybean Planting

Figure 6-1   Cold-hady rice and soybean planthy

1. 2   Significance

The value of the project is manifested in three aspects.

Firstly, it fills the gap in the cultivation and production of rice and soybean in Mongolia. Through the implementation of the project, mechanized operation and large-scale planting of soybean can be realized.

Secondly, as a traditional animal husbandry country, Mongolia is relatively backward in agriculture, particularly the cultivation of cash crops. With the development of intensive animal husbandry, the massive cultivation of corn silage will ensure supplementary feeds of livestock and the safety of livestock in winter.

Thirdly, by helping Mongolia establish cooperatives, the project has promoted China's advanced technologies. Training sessions via multiple channels has raised the awareness of local farmers and herdsmen, helped them tackle problems in reality, brought them on the same page and eventually got the common understanding across the country.

2. Cooperative Implementation

2. 1   CompletedSub-Projects

Launched in 2016, the project consists of two ten-hectare demonstration bases that were set up in Tuv Province and Orkhon Province, Mongolia respectively during 2017–2018.

At the end of 2018, the project completed the preliminary trials of three paddy rice varieties and three soybean varieties in alpine regions; 45 hectares of corn silage was planted and more than 700 tons were harvested, and the cultivation and management technologies of corn silage was basically mature; the cultivation of soybeans and forage maize was completed.

2. 2   OngoingSub-Projects

From 2019, the project started carrying out planting experiments withcold-hardy rice and soybeans in different areas across Mongolia, with an estimated investment of more than 200, 000 yuan.

2. 3   Future Plan

Next, the project will enter the stage of pilot-scale experiment. The detailed work plan is as follows.

The growing areas of soybean and paddy rice will be expanded to 500 *mu* (about 33. 3 hectares) and 100 *mu* (about 6. 7 hectares) respectively. Planting experiments will be conducted in different regions across Mongolia to accumulate experience. The growing areas of other crops will be gradually expanded as well, among which the corn silage will be increased to more than 5, 000 *mu* (about 333. 3 hectares).

3 cooperatives will be set up in Mongolia, with the recognition and support of herdsmen as much as possible.

6 training sessions will be held for leaders, scholars, farmers and herdsmen in agriculture-related fields in Mongolia. A total of 500 herdsmen (among them, women will be not less than 350) will be trained.

2 international and 2 domestic seminars will be held.

It will employ a large number of Mongolian students with study experiences in China to form a project team and pave the way for increasing its influence and facilitating the subsequent project application and implementation.

The experiment results will be widely applied to a number of counties in 5 provinces of Mongolia, including Tuv Province, Selenge Province, Darkhan-Uul Province, Khentii Province and Khovd Province, to gradually increase the planting areas of paddy rice, soybeans, corn silage and forage maize.

3. Major Characteristics

3. 1   Benefits of Cooperation

Currently, the project remains at the initial experiment stage without delivering any production benefits, but the scheduled expansion of growing areas in the coming three years promises enormous benefits.

The planned planting area of paddy rice is 1, 500mu(about 100 hectares) with a yield of 400 kg per mu. The estimated sales revenue is 2. 4 million yuan, and the estimated net revenue is 1. 2 million yuan; the planned planting area of soybean is 5, 000mu(about 333. 3 hectares) with a yield of 100 kg per mu. The estimated sales revenue is 2. 6 million yuan, and the estimated net revenue is 1. 3 million yuan; the planned planting area of corn silage is 3, 000mu(about 200 hectares) with a yield of 1, 500 kg per mu. The estimated sales revenue is 1. 2 million yuan, and the estimated net revenue is 800, 000 yuan.

In addition to economic benefits, the project will also create some local jobs:the ratio of foreign to domestic employee is 1 : 9 according to the employment policy of Mongolia, and the number of people employed by each base of the project will be more than 100 at most.

3. 2   Fields of Cooperation

The cooperation project will be expanded in the following two areas in the future: First, the planting projects of silage and soybean will be further expanded, and straw utilization projects will be carried out, so as to make up for the feed shortage in livestock and poultry industries in both China and Mongolia; Second, projects on developing the technology of growing paddy rice will be launched in deserts for expansion into new fields of research and experiments.

3.3　Influence

The project will set an example for local farmers via investigations, promotion, planting experiments and training to ensure that local farmers make full use of crop straw. Meanwhile, as winter feeds, soybean and forage maize will also provide a guarantee for local livestock to live through winter.

China's technology will be introduced into Mongolia through this project for new experiments and research based on the characteristics of local natural resources, which provides a demonstration for the development and cooperation of other agricultural technologies. Meanwhile, both sides will leverage their respective advantages in a mutually complementary manner for reciprocal and win-win results.

Case 7

Sino-Mongolia Cooperation on Scoured Cashmere Procurement

◇•

1. Project Overview

1. 1 Introduction

Founded in 1992, Viction Cashmere Group in Inner Mongolia of China is a multinational corporation group engaged in scientific research, animal husbandry, industry and trade. It primarily manufactures and sells cashmere products, with an annual output of 2, 000 tons of cashmere, 600 tons of cashmere yarn, 2 million pieces of cashmere sweaters, 2 million pieces of cashmere scarves and shawls, 500, 000 meters of woolen cashmere fabrics and 80, 000 pieces of high-quality cashmere garments. The Group is a "National Key Leading Enterprise for Agricultural Industrialization of China", one of the "Top Ten Cashmere Enterprises in China", "AAA-Credit-Level Enterprise accredited by the Ministry of Commerce of China", "Demonstrative Enterprise for China's Export Quality and Safety" accredited by the General Administration of Quality Supervision, Inspection and Quarantine of the People's Republic of China(AQSIQ), "Grade A Export Textile Enterprise", "A-level Enterprise" accredited by the General Administration of Customs of China and "National High-tech Enterprise of China".

The Group and Hun Jui LLC in Mongolia reached the following two agreements through friendly negotiations in line with the principles of equality, mutual benefit, complementary advantages, good faith and voluntariness: The procurement of 500−1, 000 tons of scoured cashmere. the project with a total investment of about 450 million yuan will be completed by the end of 2020.

1. 2 Significance

Cashmere goat is one of the special livestock varieties. Mongolia enjoys a long breeding history of raising cashmere goats and is a major cashmere producer. The cashmere industry is one of its important financial sources. The large output and low market price of cashmere make this country one of the important sources for China to import cashmere and supplement its insufficient cashmere resources.

China boasts the world's largest cashmere resources, including the world-renowned high-quality Erlangshan ("soft gold") white cashmere, Aerbasi white cashmere and Alxa white cashmere. Meanwhile, China is the world's largest producer of cashmere products, leading the international market with its production capacity of about 60% of the global output in total. In recent years, however, the influence of the ecological environment bottlenecked China's cashmere industry. This cooperation between China and Mongolia will help both sides leverage complementary advantages and jointly enhance their development of animal husbandry and processing industries.

2. Implementation

2.1   Completed Sub-Projects and Ongoing Sub-Projects

On June 27, 2019, the Viction Cashmere Group and Hun Jui LLC signed an agreement on the procurement of 1,000 tons of scoured cashmere at the Inner Mongolia(China)-Mongolia Economic and Trade Cooperation Promotion Conference.

The two companies will promote the project by fulfilling their respective responsibilities:Hun Jui LLC will be responsible for the procurement, processing, inspection, quarantine, transportation and export customs formalities of scoured cashmere among others;the Group is responsible for raising funds and examining and taking deliveries of goods.

2.2   Future Plan

Before December 31,2020,the Chinese side will raise funds of RMB

450 million for 1000 tons of scoure cashmere for Mongolia.

3. Major Characteristics

3. 1 Benefits of Cooperation

At present, the cooperation intention of the two sides has been reached, while specific business has not been launched yet. Their future cooperation will yield considerable economic benefits.

In addition, as small and medium-sized cashmere processing enterprises in Mongolia lack funds for raw cashmere procurement and technological upgrading, the signing of the agreements has enhanced mutual understanding and friendship, further advanced win-win cooperation, earnestly safeguarded bilateral interests and accordingly boosted the cooperation and development of cashmere industry between China and Mongolia.

3. 2 Fields of Cooperation

In recent years, Mongolia has paid more and more attention to increasing the capacity of the animal husbandry industry. The Government of Mongolia has formulated policy objectives in the *Action Program of the Government of Mongolia 2016−2020*, which will rapidly promote the national plan of "Mongolian Livestock" to enhance the overall economic benefits of the animal husbandry industry, establish a storage and transportation system of wool, cashmere and leather, and reserve raw materials for the processing and manufacture of livestock products.

3.3   Influence

As Mongolia has made enormous efforts to develop its animal husbandry and cashmere industries, the percentage of the cashmere industry in the primary industry will be further increased and the output of the nation's scoured cashmere and dehaired cashmere will be on the rise in a stable manner.

While contributing to China's ecological environment protection, the import of cashmere resources by Chinese enterprises will meet their production needs, further expand the output of knitted cashmere products, raise the added value and profit rates of cashmere products, and increase the export of cashmere industries. This will be another development trend of China's cashmere industry in the future.

The agreement signed by the Viction Cashmere Group and Hun Jui LLC on the procurement of 1, 000 tons of scoured cashmere has further deepened the ideas of the Sino-Mongolia bilateral economic and trade cooperation, opened up new opportunities for the exchange of products, economic complementarity and win-win cooperation.

Case 8

Sino-Russia Research on the Innovation and Utilization of Jerusalem Artichoke Resources

◇•

1. Project Overview

1. 1   Introduction

The Inner Mongolia Academy of Agricultural & Animal Husbandry Sciences of China cooperates with N. I. Vavilov Research Institute of Plant Industry or Russia to carry out research on Jerusalem artichoke resources. Their cooperation contents are as follows:

Researches are conducted on the effective integration of six common and key technologies, namely, resources exchange and innovation, variety selection and breeding, salinization improvement, desertification restoration, sanded land control, and the utilization and demonstration of Jerusalem artichoke feed; high-yield and efficient environment-friendly planting models of different types are created, and model construction standards are formulated; salinized, sandy land and forage base are constructed and restored in accordance with the technical regulations of different models; based on the improved varieties of Jerusalem artichoke, various technical measures of model integration are applied, and demonstration bases are constructed to promote the development of energy crop bases in Inner Mongolia.

1. 2　Significance

There are few resources of Jerusalem artichoke in Inner Mongolia Autonomous Region of China. Grave salinization, desertification and degradation are direct causes of wind and sandstorms in Beijing and Tianjin, while the energy plant Jerusalem artichoke is the best plant to control salinization, desertification and degradation. Therefore, Jerusalem artichoke could be used in Inner Mongolia to break the major bottlenecks of severe salinization, desertification and degradation. In addition, Jerusalem artichoke features strong cold and drought tolerance, thus research on the use of Jerusalem artichoke in tackling desertification will help solve the problems of bioenergy as well.

2. Implementation

2. 1　Completed and Ongoing Sub-Projects

At present, the two sides mainly carry out project cooperation on the following four aspects.

2. 1. 1　Studies on resource innovation, new varieties breeding and supporting cultivation techniques

Introduction, identification and screening of new varieties of special Jerusalemartichoke; introduction, identification, evaluation and breeding of the germplasm resources of special Jerusalem artichoke; selection and matching of the germplasm resources of special Jerusalem artichoke for innovation and hybrid combination.

2. 1. 2　Research on high-yield, high-efficiency and standardized cultivation techniques of the new varieties of Jerusalem artichoke grown in saline-alkalized, desertified, and sandy land

Research on high-yield, high-efficiency and standardized cultivation techniques of the new varieties of Jerusalem artichoke grown in saline-alkalized land; research on high-yield, high-efficiency and standardized cultivation techniques of the new varieties of Jerusalem artichoke grown in desertified land; research on high-yield, high-efficiency and standardized cultivation techniques of the new varieties of Jerusalem artichoke grown in sandy land; technical manual compilation of high-yield and high-efficiency cultivation of Jerusalem artichoke.

2. 1. 3　Research on the processing and utilization of Jerusalem artichoke forage

Research on the latest mowing time of Jerusalem artichoke; screening of additives suitable for silage; research on storage technology of Jerusalem artichoke cellar; research on the digestibility of Jerusalem artichoke silage; research on the usage patterns and feeding effects of Jerusalem artichoke silage.

2. 1. 4　Comprehensive technology integration, demonstration and promotion of Jerusalem artichoke

Programs of technological promotion and demonstration will be launched in several places of Inner Mongolia Autonomous Region, mainly including Togtoh County in Hohhot City, Guyang County in Baotou City, Ulanqab City and Erdos City in support of the major Jerusalem artichoke producing banners and counties.

2. 2　Future Plan

China will continue its cooperation with Russia on exchange of Jerusalem artichoke resources and materials, technological innovation and transformation, construction of demonstration parks, technology promotion, germplasm resource cultivation and other aspects.

3. Major Characteristics

3. 1　Benefits of Cooperation

3. 1. 1　Remarkable economic benefits have been achieved

During the implementation of this project, the income of Jerusalem artichoke demonstration field increased by 5. 025 million yuan. Variety improvement and nutrition regulation will help increase the output of cattle and sheep, improve the quality of livestock products and accordingly further improve the economic benefits of the breeding of cattle, sheep, pigs, chicken and ducks.

3. 1. 2　Good social benefits have been achieved

The increase of employment rates has promoted local scientific and technological breakthroughs and economic takeoff.

3. 1. 3　Good ecological benefits have been achieved

The expansion of Jerusalem artichoke planting scale and the improvement of planting technology are helpful to ease ecological problems, such as severe salinization, desertification and degradation.

3. 2　Fields of Cooperation

By means of sexual hybridization and other breeding measures, various qualified characters were integrated, and excellent varieties were found through multiple-year and multiple-generation field selections. Therefore, qualified new varieties of Jerusalem artichoke consistent with breeding goals are selected and cultivated.

To improve 2 or 3 high-yield and efficient cultivation technical regulations for Two new varieties, Khorchin Jerusalem artichoke and Mengyu No. 2 Jerusalem artichoke and other new varieties which can control the desertified, sandy and salinized land.

3. 3　Influence

This project carried out research on new varieties through scientific research cooperation between China and Russia, and promoted it on a large-scale in China. The research on science and technology between the two

sides have strengthened their bilateral technical exchanges and cooperation,
and paved the way for further cooperation in other agricultural fields. In addition, the varieties selected in this project exert diversified influences. A-
part from economic benefits, the research achievements will engender mul-
tifarious effects on ecological environment, which will play an exemplary
role in boosting bilateral ecological cooperation in the future.

Case 9

International Joint Agricultural Laboratory Project with Chinese and Russian Characteristics

◇•

1. Project Overview

1.1 Introduction

Located in the western part of Jilin Province, Baicheng Academy of Agricultural Science is geographically close to Russian agricultural development areas such as Kinov and Samara, and shares common ecological conditions and crop planting. These bring prerequisites for the establishment of the international joint laboratory and the sharing of future results.

In November 2017, Baicheng Academy of Agricultural Science of Jilin Province held talks with Russian Academy of Sciences to further strengthen the cooperative research on disease prevention and control, cultivation and processing techniques of cereal and forage crops. Relying on the cooperation platform jointly set up by the China National-Level Base for International Science and Technology Cooperation of Baicheng Academy of Agricultural Science and the Northeast Regional Center for Agricultural Sciences of Russian Academy of Sciences, the Sino-Russia Joint Laboratory has been established to integrate experts from China and Russia on cereal crops and other agricultural advantages, and carry out Sino-Russia cooperation on agricultural scientific and technological innovation. Besides, the two sides have signed the memorandum of understanding on the establishment of the Sino-Russia Center for Grain Crop Breeding, Cultivation and Processing Technology Center.

1. 2 Significance

In the context of Sino-Russia agricultural cooperation, Baicheng Academy of Agricultural Science has established a joint research platform through agricultural science and technology cooperation with a number of Russian agricultural research institutions led by the Russian Academy of Sciences. the project will promote technological breakthroughs and innovations in key areas such as the selection and breeding of new crop varieties, the integration of efficient cultivation techniques and the processing and utilization of featured agricultural products, thus jointly facilitating innovation in outstanding germplasms and technological integration and upgrading. The project will enable the two countries to engage in extensive exchange of talents, exchange of featured agricultural resources and scientific, sharing of technological resources for comprehensive expansion of cooperation areas, promotion of characteristic industries, and joint creation of internationally advanced agricultural industries. this project will also create the advantageous production areas of Coarse Cereals and Beans with Chinese and Russian Characteristics and the Distribution Center of Agricultural Products with Chinese and Russian Characteristics, promote the development of international trade and the joint training of senior talents, enhance international bilateral cooperation and mutual trust, and boost agricultural trade between China, Russia and neighboring countries.

2. Implementation

2.1 Completed and Ongoing Sub-Projects

Since 2003, Baicheng Academy of Agricultural Science has established extensive cooperation and exchanges with several Russian agricultural academies. Scientific and technological cooperation agreements have been reached with the Northeast Regional Agricultural Research Institute of Russian Academy of Sciences, the Samara Agricultural Research Institute, All-Russia Research Institute of Cereals and Beans, Tartar Agricultural Research Institute, All-Russia Feed Research Institute, Ural Agricultural Research Institute and Irkutsk Agricultural Research Institute. Their joint efforts on good variety selection and breeding, cultivation and processing technologies and other areas of oat, winter rye, buckwheat, potato, pea and other crops have yielded satisfactory results.

The large-scale promotion of the first new winter rye variety, "White BK01" jointly bred the Chinese and Russian scientists, has a profound impact on the research and development of new winter rye products, the innovation of processing technology, ecological environmental protection, the upgrading of characteristic industries and the expansion of Sino-Russia trade channels.

2.2   Future Plan

In the future, the two sides will conduct further cooperation in the following areas.

First, joint innovation of the germplasm resources of featured crops. Russia is located in a high-latitude region with a vast territory, large longitude span, complex ecological environment, diverse types of crop resources, most of which are characterized by strong stress resistance, good yield stability and excellent quality. Many extraordinary genes are not available in China's existing resources. Therefore, it is one of the key tasks of Smo-Russia laboratory to introduce and utilize different types of variety resources in a targeted manner, and integrate them with China's excellent domestic resources through the process of introduction, digestion, absorption and re-innovation.

Second, the joint innovation of new varieties of featured crops. This project will help strengthen contacts and exchanges with scientific research institutions of relevant countries. By hiring experts, sending personnel for studies abroad and other means, the project will introduce breeding techniques and methods, integrate them with the advantages and characteristics of China's featured crop resources, and make use of the talent advantages of the system. In addition, it will improve China's breeding system with China's characteristics in light of the diverse natural ecological conditions in China to guide crop breeding with Chinese characteristics.

Third, integrated innovation of characteristic crop cultivation technology. The physiological characteristics of different crops will be explored, and adaptability tests and gene-environment interaction tests in different regions will be carried out. China's natural and production conditions and production development trends will be considered to develop appropriate cultivation techniques and measures, and earnestly carry out researches on supporting cultivation techniques in view of the innovation of characteristic crop varieties. Specific measures include cultivation physiological research, planting pattern research, mechanized production technology and other integrated technology integration and innovation research.

3. Major Characteristics

3.1 Benefits of Cooperation

The joint laboratory will make full use of the excellent oat resources abroad, carry out international scientific and technological cooperation and in-depth scientific researches, and rapidly improve China's independent innovation capability, in order to break the bottlenecks in the development of agricultural industry in the western region of Jilin Province, and promote industrial progress in related fields.

By means of joint construction, the project will explore multi-angle and multi-field technology integration and joint product development at home and abroad, promote the internationalization process of China's oat research and development, create an international development model featured by technology integration, test demonstration, and joint development, and provide technical and talent support for the leap-forward development of oat in China.

3.2   Fields of Cooperation

With the strategic thinking of key breakthroughs and radiating overall effect, the project will pay attention to the advantages of capital, technology and talent to enhance the extensive and in-depth cooperation between China and Russia in agricultural scientific research and development, agro-ecological protection and management, organic agricultural product cultivation as well as advanced agricultural product processing technology.

The establishment of the joint laboratory and demonstrative Sino-Russia scientific research base will render technical support and services for the agricultural development of China and Russia, and promote the green and sustainable agricultural development of the countries along the BRI routes(the Belt and Road).

3.3   Influence

The demonstration effect of the project is mainly reflected in the following aspects.

First, It can jointly promote the overall improvement of Sino-Russia agricultural scientific and technological innovation capability. Based on the extensive cooperation between China and Russia in agriculture, the International Joint Agricultural Laboratory with Chinese and Russian Characteristics combines the existing agricultural research advantages and development needs of the two countries, carries out targeted technology integration and technology resource sharing, and jointly launches experiments to develop scientific and technological synergy. It will greatly promote the substantial improvement of innovation capability of both countries in related fields.

Second, It can drive the formation and development of the agricultural dominant areas with Chinese and Russian characteristics. The International Joint Laboratory is the integration and re-innovation of the existing bilateral cooperation. And the scientific research results will be highly consistent with the actual development of agriculture. Therefore, this project will definitely support the development of agriculture with their own characteristics and form their advantages in agricultural development, and drive the improvement of their comprehensive agricultural production capacity.

Third, besides, this project will also enhance Sino-Russia agricultural industrial cooperation and joint development. The establishment of the international joint laboratory will not only devote to planting research, but also extend to product research and development. Relevant processing and industrialization achievements will promote the progress of characteristic agricultural industry through transformation, and stimulate the joint participation enterprises of both sides. It is expected to form a Sino-Russian

agricultural economic linkage system with processing results as the bond,
joint production bases as support, enterprises as the driving force, and the
development of a series characteristic products as the goal.

Case 10

Agricultural Plantation Project in Jewish Autonomous Oblast(Yevreyskaya Avtonomnaya Oblast) of Russia

◇•

1. Project Overview

1.1 Introduction

North Agricultural Company of Jewish Autonomous Oblast, Russia (herein refered to as North Company) is a wholly-Sino-funded company incorporated in 2013. With a registered capital of RUR 33 million, the company is invested by Qindeli Farm Baolong Fishery Co., Ltd., registered in Birobidzhan.

The company has leased more than 20, 000 hectares of agricultural land from the governments of Nizhneleninskoye and Birobidzhan and other Russian agricultural companies, to cary out agricultural plantation project, and has invested more than 60 million yuan in total.

1. 2   Significance

The company has established long-term and stable cooperative relations with grain enterprises in Japan, Canada, Australia, South Korea, North Korea and other countries, which plays an important role in establishing a multi-party cooperation.

Together with Heilongjiang Provincial Academy of Agricultural Sciences, the company has established a scientific and technological experiment and demonstration base in Russia, for the plantation of a variety of crops, such as soybean, corn, paddy rice, wheat, potato, and ginseng. With the help of the industry-university-research platform, it can make full use of local resources to develop new varieties.

2. Implementation

2. 1   Completed and Ongoing Sub-Projects

North Agrialltaral Company of Jewish Autonomous Oblast, Russia is the largest wholly-Chinese-funded agricultural enterprise in Jewish Autonomous Oblast of Russia and also the largest wholly-owned planting enterprise in the Far East. Having been operated in the Jewish Autonomous Oblast for six consecutive years, the company has achieved considerable economic and social benefits.

Sofar, The company has invested in the building of water conservancy, road and supporting facilities of 15, 000-hectare land, including cement culvert manufacturing plants, drying towers and paddy rice processing plants. It has reclaimed 15, 000 hectares of wasteland, and planted soybean, paddy rice, corn, wheat and other crops on it with an annual grain output of 40, 000 tons.

North company, in cooperation with the Chinese Academy of Agricultural Sciences of Heilongjiang, has set up a science and technology demonstration park, where good varieties of crops such as wheat, corn, soybean, oil flax and forage grass have been planted in trial. In 2019, North Company newly introduced Ginseng planting and established a Ginseng planting and seedling base.

The company has signed a long-term agricultural product procurement contract with General Co., Ltd, Bank of Hokkaido, of Japan, signed a strategic cooperation agreement with CBH Company of Australia, engaged in grain trade with Mt. Walbong Company of North Korea, established friendly cooperative relationship with the National Agricultural Cooperative Federation(Korea Nonghyup) of South Korea, and signed an contract in agricultural product sales with Royal Classical Agriculture Ltd. of Canada.

2. 2 Future Plan

In the future, the company will focus on the following aspects: Continue to expand the scale of planting into four planting sectors of vegetables, food crops, forage grass and oil crops. Leverage Russia's existing supportive policies for the breeding industry to achieve added value of grain. Engage in the integrated operation of storage, processing and logistics of grains. By leveraging the low cost of Russian agricultural products, it will render the products to the international grain market.

3. Major Characteristics

3.1   Benefits of Cooperation

Since its establishment, the company has been strictly operating in accordance with the laws and regulations of Russia. The company has an elite management team of 9 Russian executives and employs more than 100 local workers from Russia, which registers a decent contribution to the local employment situation. in addition, The company has more than 100 sets of large agricultural machinery such as Case, John Deere and other brands. It has reclaimed 15, 000 hectares of wasteland and partially passed international organic food origin certification, which has greatly contributed to the development of local agriculture.

3.2   Fields of Cooperation

In the future, the company will establish a close cooperative relationship with Yingkou Area of China(Liaoning) Pilot Free Trade Zone. Via the Tongjiang Railway Bridge, the two sides will establish a channel of grain logistics from Russia to Yingkou Port in China, which makes it possible to ship the grain produced in the Russian Far East via Yingkou Port to the processing plants in the coastal cities in China at low cost. It will cooperate with large domestic agricultural enterprises in China to build another grain base of the same size as the Jiansanjiang Reclamation Area in Jewish Autonomous Oblast.

3. 3　Influence

It plays an exemplary and guiding role for small-and-medium-sized agricultural enterprises in China, and introduces its successful experience to Chinese enterprises aiming for agricultural operations in the Russian Far East. It offers technical guidance to the surrounding Russian farms in cultivation technology and using of agricultural machinery, which not only increases their production and technology capability, but also makes it possible for the multiple parties thus involved to forge partnerships by virtue of their advantages. As a publicity and display base for the local government, the enterprise has attracted visitors from agricultural companies of Japan, South Korea, Vietnam, Canada and Australia and become a model for the local agricultural development.

Trade and Investment

Case 11

Sino-Mongolia Cooperation for
Trade in Layer Feeds and Wheat Bran

◇·◇

1. Project Overview

1.1   Introduction

Established in April 2000 in Inner Mongolia Autonomous Region, China, Baotou City Bei Chen Feed Technology Co., Ltd. is a national key leading enterprise for agricultural industrialization, a national high-tech enterprise, a board member of China Feed Industry Association(CFIA), one of the first pilot enterprises of traceable green food across China and a Demonstrative Enterprise for the Administrative Specifications on Feed Quality Safety of the Ministry of Agriculture and Rural Affairs of China(See Figure 11-1). In recent years, the company has followed the path of combining domestic and foreign trade, and actively developed trade relations with enterprises in Mongolia.

a. Warehouse of Finished Products

b. Warehouse

c. Stacking by Robot

Figue 11-1　The interior of Beichen Feed Technology Co., Ltd., Baoton City, Inner Mongolia Autonomous Region, China

(Source of the Photo: the Chinese side of the Cooperation Program)

At present, the cooperation between Chinese and Mongolia is as follows: Trade of layer feeds with AJIGANA LLC in Ulaanbaatar, Mongolia; trade of layer feeds with Tumen Shuvuut Co., Ltd., in Ulaanbaatar, Mongolia; import of wheat bran from Mongolia through other Chinese enterprises.

The implementation of multilateral import and export cooperation projects has made positive contribution to the win-win and mutually complementary development of Chinese and Mongolian enterprises.

1. 2   Significance

Mongolia is rich in agriculture and animal husbandry resources and has huge potential of agricultural products. However, it is a latecomer in the development of the processing industry, whose technology falls behind. China has advantages in technology to some extent, but isk not well endowed with resources; The combination of China's advanced processing technologies with the rich agricultural resources of Mongolia is of great significance to the economic growth of both sides and has huge development potential for both sides.

2. Implementation

2. 1   Completed and Ongoing Sub-Projects

Bei Chen Feed Technology Co., Ltd., Baotou City, Inner Mongolia Autonomous Region, China has signed a trade cooperation agreement with AJIGANA LLC and Tumen Shuvuut Co., Ltd. in Ulaanbaatar, Mongolia on layer feed export to Mongolia continuously from 2010.

The company began importing wheat bran from Mongolia through Inner Mongolia Ronghao Import & Export Trade Co., Ltd. since 2010.

2. 2   Future Plan

The next step of Bei Chen Feed Technology Co. , Ltd. , is as follows.

It will further expand the trade with Mongolia by increasing the export volume and value of layer, cattle and sheep feed, strive to reach 20, 000 tons and USD 10 million respectively in three years. It will further increase the import volume and value of wheat bran and other agricultural products for the targets of 12, 000 tons and USD 3 million respectively in three years.

3. Major Characteristics

3. 1   Benefits of Cooperation

From 2010 to 2017, Bei Chen Feed Technology Co. , Ltd. annually exported 6, 800 tons of layer feed to Tumen Shuvuut Co. , Ltd. , with a total export value of about USD 3. 2 million on average. The profit of feed is 150 yuan each ton on average and 1. 02 million yuan (approximately USD 150, 000) each year.

The company has cooperated with AJIGANA co. , Ltd. since 2018 on the export of layer feed to Mongolia. It annually exports 7, 500 tons of layer feed with a total export value of USD 3. 5 million on average. The profit of the feeds averages 200 yuan each ton and 1. 5 million yuan (approximately USD 230, 000) each year.

The company began importing wheat bran from Mongolia in 2010 with the annual average import volume and value of about 4, 000 tons and USD 800, 000. The profit of the import averages 100 yuan each ton, namely, 400, 000 yuan for the 4, 000 tons of wheat bran in total.

3. 2   Fields of Cooperation

At present, based on the solid collaboration over the past nine years, Bei Chen Feed Technology Co., Ltd. has established good and stable business partnerships with many Mongolia-based enterprises in layer feed. In the future, the parties involved will strengthen business exchanges, expand the scope of trade and boost multilateral cooperation mechanisms.

3. 3   Influence

The implementation of cooperation project will help to promote the development of large-scale trade in relevant industries and drive relevant enterprises to pursue deep integration and mutually beneficial growth, thus creating favorable conditions for enterprises on both sides to engage in joint investment and construction for stable development in agriculture.

Case 12

Feed Trade Project between
China and Mongolia

◇•

1. Project Overview

1.1 Introduction

Liaoning Wellhope Agri-Tech Joint Stock Co., Ltd. (Wellhope) is a national leading enterprise in agricultural industrialization of China, a vice-president entity of China Feed Industry Association and that of China Animal Agriculture Association concurrently.

Due to Mongolia's vast territory and sparse population, long winter duration, and natural stocking-based animal husbandry, large-scale and modern production is difficult to achieve in a short time. Based on the factors mentioned above, Wellhope exported layer feed and feed raw material products to Mongolia from 2014, offer regular technical services and organize technical exchanges for Mongolian customers.

1.2   Significance

Wellhope has established standardized breeding communities in Mongolia according to livestock categories and local characteristics, and carried out scientific management on breeding equipment, feeding patterns and feed applications, and played a demonstration role for local farmers (See Figure 12-1).

a. Workshop   b. Chicken Farm

**Figure 12-1   Workshop and Chicken form of Liaoning
Wellhope Agri-Tech Joint Stock Co., Ltd.**

(Source of the Photos: the Chinese side of the Cooperation Program)

The project can provide professional technical services and training for local farmers, and guide farmers to accept the changes of feeding patterns through the popularization and dissemination of professional knowledge and economic benefit analysis, which can improve the overall level of livestock breeding in Mongolia.

The implementation of this project will facilitate the rapid development of Wellhope's business in Mongolian market and increase its influence and market share in Mongolia.

2. Implementation

2.1 Completed and Ongoing Sub-Projects

At present, Wellhope cooperates with its Mongolia partners in the following aspects.

First, promoting direct investment through trade, they look for partners with sufficient strength in Mongolia to set up joint ventures on feed processing, livestock and poultry breeding, slaughtering and processing or other business activities(See Figure 12-2).

Second, the advanced technology and management experience of Wellhope are applied to the market development and project management in Mongolia, and scientific and technological achievements are transformed into productivity. They provide customers with training and services to enhance the overall development level of animal husbandry in Mongolia.

Third, train full-time technical service personnel locally, train customers through seminars, publicize advanced feeding models and feeding management knowledge to change the breeding concepts in Mongolia.

**Figure 12-2   Products sold by Liaoning Wellhope Agri-Tech
Joint Customers in Mongolia of Stock Co., Ltd.**

(Source of the Photo: the Chinese side of the Cooperation Program)

2.2   Future Plan

In the future, Wellhope hopes to carry out cooperation with local large-scale breeding enterprises with sufficient strength in the following aspects.

First, the processing of high-quality feeds, modern scientific feeding model in Mongolia. It aims to help breeding farmers to change the traditional breeding concepts, gradually forming large-scale farming, improving breeding performance, and then increasing their economic benefits.

Second, broiler industrialization. Wellhope's overseas investment experience and professional technical and management advantages will be made full use of to carry out industrialized broiler businesses, including breeding, hatching, slaughtering and food processing.

Third, mongolian beef and mutton import business. The number of cattle and sheep is large, with high cost performance and palatable flesh. In the past two years, cooked meat products have already been exported to China. Wellhope will pay close attention to the policies of both countries on the trade of Mongolian meat products, and carry out trade business of meat products in a timely manner.

3. Major Characteristics

3.1 Benefits of Cooperation

Although the total amount of cattle and sheep breeding is large in Mongolia, the industry is at the primary stage. Laying hens is relatively mature in a large scale. The number of broiler and pig is relatively small, and the feeding level and breeding performance are mediocre. However, since the local people favor fresh chicken and pork, the industrialization of livestock and poultry breeding is endowed with great development potential.

As livestock breeding in Mongolia lags behind and had not formed large-scale farms, the industrialization of feed and livestock breeding industries is far from mature. In Mongolia, the feed mills are small in both number and scale, and their simple processing techniques are mostly used as supporting means for local breeding farms. In addition, since the feedstuff is made of single raw material and mostly imported, the feed cost is high and technical formulation capability is low. Therefore, the overall breeding performance is quite poor in Mongolia.

By carrying out export trade, Wellhope hopes to promote investment in the Mongolian market, develop potential customer resources, seek partners with admirable strength. Cooperation in the fields of feed, breeding, slaughtering and processing can enhance the further development of Mongolia's animal husbandry industry, and achieve economic benefits.

3.2   Fields of Cooperation

The implementation of this project will promote the business development of Wellhope in Mongolian market and increase its influence and market share in Mongolia, so that the company can promote the development of Mongolia's animal husbandry industry; it will expand the business scope of Wellhope and then increase its economic benefits in the Mongolian market. In addition to the feed sector, the project will also be expanded to feed raw materials, breeding and slaughtering sectors. The implementation of this project will play a demonstrative role in improving the local feed processing level, facilitating the change of breeding concepts, and introducing modern breeding methods, thereby improving the overall development level of Mongolia's animal husbandry industry. The project will create more jobs for local people. Through large-scale breeding, advanced management and modern slaughtering methods, the project will ensure the food quality and safety such as meat, eggs and milk.

3.3 Influence

Animal husbandry is not only an industry related to the national economy and people's livelihood, but also a sunrise industry. For Mongolia, in particular, it is an economic pillar industry with enormous development potential and great significance; the implementation of this project will upgrade Mongolia's overall breeding concept and enable the country to gradually adopt scientific breeding patterns, so as to increase the output of meat, eggs and milk, promote the development of the feed industry and facilitate the rapid development of livestock and poultry industrialization; the problems concerning the food safety of Mongolia's livestock products will be effectively addressed by means of modern breeding methods and management modes, regulating the key links of livestock and poultry breeding in Mongolia, such as the management and addition of drugs, the use of vaccines and the supervision of health indicators, etc.

Case 13

Korea International Cooperation
Agency Cooperation Project in Mongolia

◇•

1. Cooperation with KOICA

KOICA Mongolia Office is an overseas branch of KOICA (Korea International Cooperation Agency).

KOICA was founded in 1991. As a government agency, KOICA is committed to maximizing the effectiveness of Korea's grant aid programs for developing countries by implementing the Korean government's grant aid and technical cooperation programs.

As Mongolia was selected as a "priority development country" by KOICA, KOICA's aid volume to Mongolia has increased steadily. KOICA Mongolia Office provided USD 9. 8859 billion in assistance between 1991 and 2011.

Currently, four types of assistance projects are being implemented by the KOICA Mongolia Office: Project Aid, Training Program, World Friends Korea Program and Partnership with NGOs. All four types are based on the MDGs in order to ensure effective implementation.

2. Cooperative Implementation

The following projects are successfully implemented in the field of agriculture and animal husbandry in Mongolia(See Table 13-1).

Table 13-1   Successful cases in the field

Project title	Content	Budget
Agriculture and Livestock farming in Khalkhgol agricultural zone	Office facilities, 190 sguare meter hay warehouse and 1, 950 sguare meter of intensive beef warehouse, 525 sguare meter of intensive dairy factory Zimmatic brand irrigation system for 155ha of farmland for livestock feed and plant breeding three 70×5-meters green houses for growing underground plants Infrastructure construction within 13 km. Underground wells/borehole Human resources development Equipment supply	USD 4. 0 million
The Reconstruction of the Mongolia State Central Veterinary Laboratory of Mongolia	Human resources development Equipment supply	USD 13. 0 million- 16. 0 million

Case 14

Jimeng International Cooperation Park for Ecological Agriculture and Animal Husbandry

◇•

1. Project Overview

1.1   Introduction

China's Jilin Jimeng Agriculture and Animal Husbandry Industry Development Co., Ltd. (Jimeng) was established on November 20, 2015, with a registered capital of 100 million yuan. Its main business includes ecological and organic agricultural cultivation, green ecological animal husbandry, the production, processing, import and export of agricultural and animal husbandry products and so on.

In 2016, Jimeng obtained the land use right of 25, 000 hectares of agricultural land and 120 hectares of construction land in Tumentsogt County,

Sukhbaatar Province, Mongolia. it plans to invest USD 120 million to build "Jilin-Mongolia International Cooperation Park for Ecological Agriculture and Animal Husbandry" (See Figure 14-1, 14-2).

Figure 14-1   Pasture and Cattle of the Company

(Source of the Photos: the Chinese side of the Cooperation Program)

1. 2   Significance

Generally speaking, the implementation of "Jilin-Mongolia International Cooperation Park for Ecological Agriculture and Animal Husbandry" will generate value in many aspects, mainly including:

First, The promotion of technology. The construction of the park will greatly facilitate the promotion of green agricultural planting and harmless animal husbandry technology in Mongolia.

Figure 14-2   Ploughed Land

(Source of the Photos: the Chinese side of the Cooperation Program)

Second, Environmental protection. A green ecological agriculture project and a traditional green animal husbandry project will be carried out in the park. The implementation of the projects will play an important role in the protection of the local natural environment and ecosystem.

Third, Local employment. The project currently employs 55 local herdsmen. In the "Company + Herdsman" model, 350 Mongolian herdsmen will realize common prosperity in the future.

Fourth, Industrial integration. The park will further develop and implement eco-tourism projects. It will further promote the local economic development by incorporating leisure agriculture and eco-tourism into traditional agriculture and animal husbandry.

2. Implementation

2. 1   Completed and Ongoing Sub-Projects

So far, part of the preliminary preparations for the project have been partially completed, such as investment and construction, agreement signing, land transfer and facility construction.

45 million yuan has been paid for the land purchase.

It has obtained the approval documents from Mongolian Government and Jilin Provincial Government and has completed the filing of the Development and Reform Commission of Changchun Economic and Technological Development Zone, the Development and Reform Commission of Changchun Municipality and the Development and Reform Commission of Jilin Province, and submitted an application to the National Development and Reform Commission of China.

It has obtained the land inspection report and the climate inspection report of the Jimeng International Cooperation Park for Ecological Agriculture and Animal Husbandry, signed the Mongolian land transfer contract, obtained the land certificate, business license and land mapping, and confirmed the Company + Household(herdsman)cooperation intention letters.

Part of the land in the park has been ploughed and leveled. Nearly 20 types of agricultural products have been planted on trial basis(See Figure 14-3)and 60, 000 *mu*(4, 000 hectares)of oat grass have been planted. The park currently raises 5, 000 cattle and 20, 000 sheep.

a. A Good Harvest of Oat Grass   b. Beet Trial Garden

Figure 14-3   Plantings in the park

(Source of the Photo:the Chinese side of the Cooperation Program)

The examination and approval procedures for 120 hectares of construction land have been completed, the land use certificate has been issued, fences have been built around 120 hectares of construction land, temporary offices and living quarters have been set up.

2. 2   Future Plan

In the future, the project will focus on the following issues.

First, investment and financing. On the basis of existing infrastructure, the project contents will be continuously expanded through investment and financing so as to promote the diversified development of the project. However, there are difficulties in financing owing to the high risk, long investment cycle, and slow return of investment in agriculture, which shall be addressed as priorities in the future.

Second, park infrastructure improvement and consolidation. On the basis of protecting the local ecological environment, infrastructure construction will be improved according to the needs of the projectso as to lay a solid foundation for its subsequent development.

Third, market research and project potential assessment. Preparations need to be made for the specific implementation of the future project.

Fourth, domestic quotas application. Domestic quotas of agricultural products will be shipped back to China, especially those of the oat produced abroad by the company.

3. Major Characteristics

3.1 Benefits of Cooperation

Some specific contents of this project involve the production and processing of raw agricultural products and animal husbandry products. And the project will create trademarks and brands with the theme of "the Kherlen River". On the one hand, this will promote the development of local agricultural and animal product processing industries; on the other hand, resource products will be shipped back to China, which will further enrich China's domestic agricultural product supply.

Another specific content of this project is about the development of grassland ecotourism, which will not only contribute to the local ecological environment protection from the market perspective, but also provide a good model for the comprehensive development of local agriculture and animal husbandry.

3.2   Fields of Cooperation

Rich in resources, Mongolia enjoys the advantages for the development of green ecological agriculture. Based on Mongolia's natural resource advantages, this project will combine Mongolia's natural resources and make full use of the pollution-free land, water sources to develop green ecological agriculture.

In the model of "Company + Herdsman" cooperation, this project provides free pastures to the herdsmen in the surrounding areas. The development of traditional green animal husbandry will further promote the sound circle development of the project.

3.3   Influence

Centered on production and processing, this market-oriented project stays in tune with the concept of greening, environmental protection and sustainable development. It can provide a model for the construction of the local industry chains of ecological agriculture and animal husbandry.

The project combines planting and animal husbandry in the primary industry with leisure agriculture and eco-tourism in the tertiary industry, breaks the original industrial development model, and enhances the value of agricultural and animal husbandry products. It has a good impact on the increase in production and income of local farmers and herdsmen.

The project is dedicated to building a brand for high-quality green products and establishing an international-level demonstrative park in Mongolia. With China's implementation of the Belt and Road Initiative, it enhances the cooperation between the two countries in agricultural and animal husbandry production and trade and serves as a model for other Chinese enterprises to seek partnerships along the BRI routes(the Belt and the Road).

Case 15

Chinese Agricultural Product Distribution Center in Russia

◇·

1. Project Overview

1.1 Introduction

In 2016, Manzhouli De Feng Trade Co., Ltd. founded Lewkenner Private LLC in Irkutsk, Russia with a registered capital of USD 350,000 and invested more than 5 million yuan to build a cross-border agricultural products distribution center in Russia.

The project has effectively improved the cross-border sales and service level of agricultural products, boosted the market competitiveness and influence of fruits and vegetables in the Russian Far East, won the trust and praise of local consumers, and promoted vegetable farmers to increase both production and income.

1. 2 Significance

China boasts abundant agricultural products in complete varieties. Given the protracted freezing winter in Russia, its agricultural product market is under supplied, particularly the relatively high demand for fruits and vegetables. Although the transportation is convenient in winter, improper storage of fruit and vegetable would cause severe frost damage. The implementation of this project has realized the complementarity of agricultural products of the two countries.

By investing in the cross-border agricultural product storage and distribution centers, this project has not only effectively reduced the losses caused by improper storage of exported agricultural products, but also lowered the local labor costs.

2. Implementation

2. 1 Completed Sub-Projects

In 2016, Manzhouli De Feng Trade Co., Ltd. (based in Inner Mongolia, China) founded the locally incorporated entity, Lewkenner Private LLC in Irkutsk, Russia. Currently, the company has invested more than 5 million yuan for the construction of a cross-border agricultural product distribution center.

2. 2   OngoingSub-Projects

In June 2018, Manzhouli De Feng Trade Co., Ltd. invested another 853, 000 yuan. The main structure of 304 square meters of constant temperature fresh-keeping warehouse and the main structure of 575 square meters of fruit and vegetable processing and distribution center have been completed, and the light steel roof truss is being manufactured and installed.

2. 3   Future Plan

Efforts will be made toenhance the project construction, promote the rapid growth and healthy and sustainable development of Manzhouli's export trade to Russia, push the Sino-Russia fruit and vegetable import, export and processing industry to a new height, and promote the development of agricultural enterprises to pursue large-scale, scientific, and industrialization.

3. Major Characteristics

3. 1   Benefits of Cooperation

At present, the distribution center has an annual turnover of 50, 000 tons of fruits and vegetables. After the project is put into operation in 2018, the annual profit is expected to increase by 1. 8 million yuan. Considering the average annual cost of 1. 05 million yuan, the total incremental profit will be 750, 000 yuan.

3. 2　Fields of Cooperation

This project represents an organic combination of the processing, production and recycling of resources and will help increase the total volume of bilateral trade in the Manzhouli region, thereby giving a strong boost to the vigorous development of the Chinese Russian in the region. The development of this project has enhanced the development of the other related industries in the region, increased employment opportunities and local people's incomes, and played a positive role in social stability, local people's prosperity and socialist economic development.

3. 3　Influence

The project will promote the development of fruit and vegetable bases across China. At present, more than 40 bases have been involved. It will bring the advantages of local resources around China into full play so as to develop local agricultural economy. This project has both admirable economic benefits and social ones, which meets the requirements for the sustainable development of the agricultural economy. After the project is put into operation, it can work in tandem with the development of industrial, economic, humanistic, social and other sectors, and adapt to the surrounding social environment.

Case 16

Projects of Wellhope
Agri-Tech Company in Russia

◇•

1. Project Overview

1. 1   Introduction

China's Liaoning Wellhope Agri-Tech Joint Stock Co., Ltd. (Well-hope) is a national leading enterprise in agricultural industrialization, a vice-president entity of China Feed Industry Association and that of China Animal Agriculture Association concurrently.

In 2018, Wellhope and Russia IVA LLC established Russia Wellhope Agri-Tech Company, a joint venture in the border city of Pokrovka in Okty-abrsky District of Primorsky Krai. It is not only the nearest overseas indus-trial park to China, but also a demonstrative overseas industrial park of Heilongjiang-Russia cooperation.

The total planning area is 4 square kilometers, the land area with completed legal procedures for the industrial park is 3. 6 square kilometers, and the floor area with those procedures is 135, 000 square meters.

1. 2   Significance

As one of the countries along the Belt and Road(the BRI), Russia is an important object of China's foreign direct investment. The two countries are geographically adjacent, culturally connected and complementary in resources, thus have huge investment potential.

The investment location of the project is Ussuriysk of Primorsky Krai, Russia, where mature feed enterprises, big and highly profitable pig farms and layer farms are relatively insufficient. According to the strategic plan of Russia Wellhope, the company is to develop into a feed producer, and carry out pig and layer breeding business and feed raw material business to provide local people with high-quality pork products and eggs for the benefit of society.

It will supply feedstuff for surrounding farms and self-operated farms (See Figure 16-1), save resources, protect environment and improve the economic benefits of breeding.

2. Implementation

2. 1   Completed and Ongoing Sub-Projects

In 2018, Wellhope and IVA LLC established Russia Wellhope Agri-Tech Company, a joint venture, and its main businesses include production

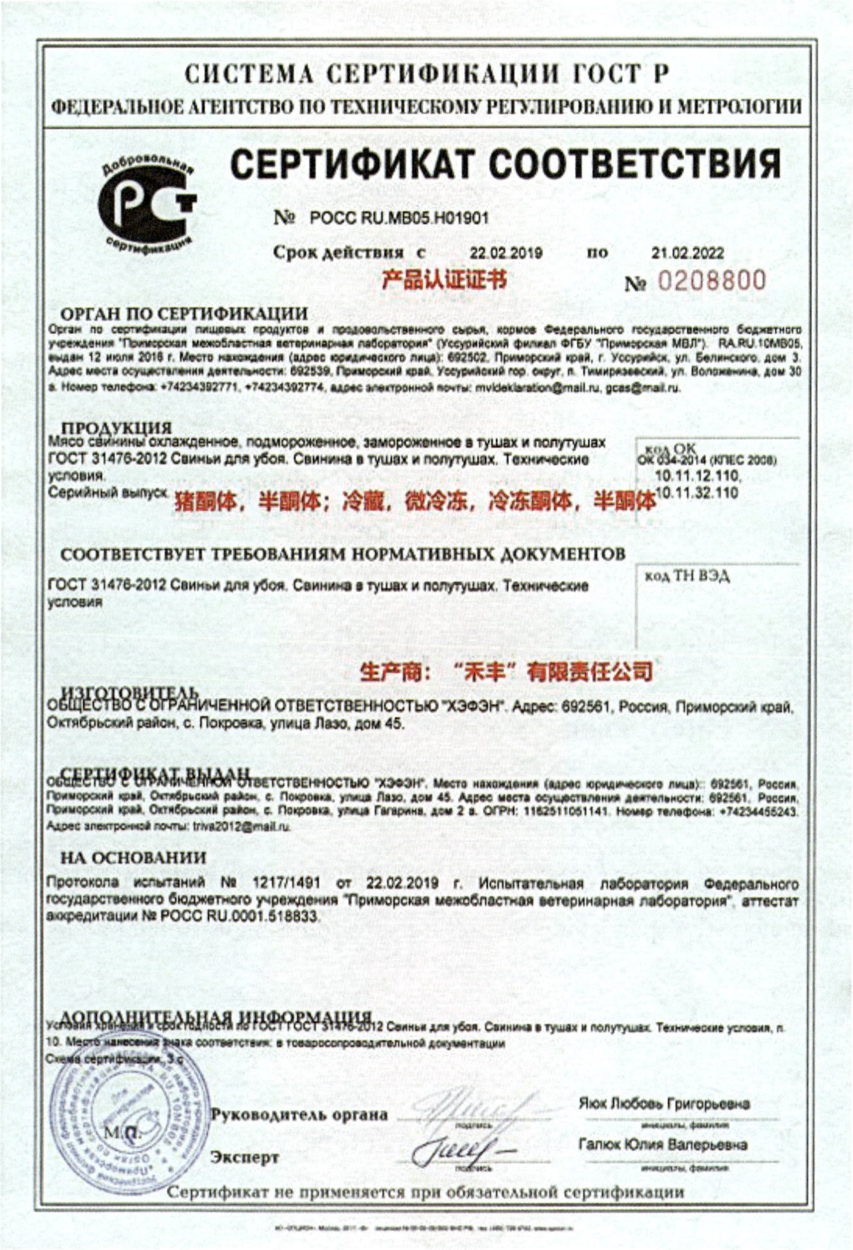

СИСТЕМА СЕРТИФИКАЦИИ ГОСТ Р

ФЕДЕРАЛЬНОЕ АГЕНТСТВО ПО ТЕХНИЧЕСКОМУ РЕГУЛИРОВАНИЮ И МЕТРОЛОГИИ

Добровольная сертификация

СЕРТИФИКАТ СООТВЕТСТВИЯ

№ РОСС RU.MB05.H01901

Срок действия с 22.02.2019 по 21.02.2022

产品认证证书 № 0208800

ОРГАН ПО СЕРТИФИКАЦИИ

Орган по сертификации пищевых продуктов и продовольственного сырья, кормов Федерального государственного бюджетного учреждения "Приморская межобластная ветеринарная лаборатория" (Уссурийский филиал ФГБУ "Приморская МВЛ"). RA.RU.10MB05, выдан 12 июля 2016 г. Место нахождения (адрес юридического лица): 692502, Приморский край, г. Уссурийск, ул. Белинского, дом 3. Адрес места осуществления деятельности: 692539, Приморский край, Уссурийский гор. округ, п. Тимирязевский, ул. Воложенина, дом 30 а. Номер телефона: +74234392771, +74234392774, адрес электронной почты: mvldeklaration@mail.ru, gcas@mail.ru.

ПРОДУКЦИЯ

Мясо свинины охлажденное, подмороженное, замороженное в тушах и полутушах ГОСТ 31476-2012 Свиньи для убоя. Свинина в тушах и полутушах. Технические условия.

Серийный выпуск. 猪酮体，半酮体；冷藏，微冷冻，冷冻酮体，半酮体

код ОК
ОК 034-2014 (КПЕС 2008)
10.11.12.110,
10.11.32.110

СООТВЕТСТВУЕТ ТРЕБОВАНИЯМ НОРМАТИВНЫХ ДОКУМЕНТОВ

ГОСТ 31476-2012 Свиньи для убоя. Свинина в тушах и полутушах. Технические условия

код ТН ВЭД

生产商："禾丰"有限责任公司

ИЗГОТОВИТЕЛЬ

ОБЩЕСТВО С ОГРАНИЧЕННОЙ ОТВЕТСТВЕННОСТЬЮ "ХЭФЭН". Адрес: 692561, Россия, Приморский край, Октябрьский район, с. Покровка, улица Лазо, дом 45.

СЕРТИФИКАТ ВЫДАН

ОБЩЕСТВО С ОГРАНИЧЕННОЙ ОТВЕТСТВЕННОСТЬЮ "ХЭФЭН", Место нахождения (адрес юридического лица): 692561, Россия, Приморский край, Октябрьский район, с. Покровка, улица Лазо, дом 45. Адрес места осуществления деятельности: 692561, Россия, Приморский край, Октябрьский район, с. Покровка, улица Гагарина, дом 2 в. ОГРН: 1162511061141. Номер телефона: +7423445524З. Адрес электронной почты: triva2012@mail.ru.

НА ОСНОВАНИИ

Протокола испытаний № 1217/1491 от 22.02.2019 г. Испытательная лаборатория Федерального государственного бюджетного учреждения "Приморская межобластная ветеринарная лаборатория", аттестат аккредитации № РОСС RU.0001.518833.

ДОПОЛНИТЕЛЬНАЯ ИНФОРМАЦИЯ

Условия хранения и срок годности по ГОСТ ГОСТ 31476-2012 Свиньи для убоя. Свинина в тушах и полутушах. Технические условия, п. 10. Место нанесения знака соответствия: в товаросопроводительной документации

Схема сертификации: 3с

М.П.

Руководитель органа ______ подпись Яюк Любовь Григорьевна инициалы, фамилия

Эксперт ______ подпись Галюк Юлия Валерьевна инициалы, фамилия

Сертификат не применяется при обязательной сертификации

Figure 16-1 Product Certification

(Source of the Photos: the Chinese side of theCooperation Program)

and sales of feed and feed additives, grain cultivation, acquisition and trade, sales of feedstuff, poultry and livestock breeding, etc.

The total investment of this project is 28 million yuan (approximately USD 4. 1056 million at the exchange rate of 6. 82 yuan per dollar), of which, Wellhope invests 15. 4 million yuan (approximately USD 2. 2581 million at the exchange rate of 6. 82 yuan per dollar), accounting for 55% of the shares; the Russian company invests 12. 6 million yuan in the form of biological assets (approximately USD 1. 8475 million at the exchange rate of 6. 82 yuan per dollar), accounting for 45% of the shares.

The project is located in Primorsky Krai, Russia. At present, the joint venture leases pig and layer farms (See Figure 16−2) and feed mills (See Fugyre 16−3) to carry out related businesses.

2. 2　Future Plan

Plan for the next three years: build a new premix plant to carry out the production and sales of commercial feed; renovate and build new pig farms and henneries, expand the scale of breeding, and improve the efficiency of breeding.

3. Major Characteristics

3. 1　Benefits of Cooperation

The implementation of this project will change the local breeding pat-

a. Pig Farm   b. Layer Farm

Figure 16-2   Rented pigfarm and layer farm of Russia Wellhope Agri-Tech Company
(Source of the Photos: the Chinese side of the Cooperation Program)

terns and improve the economic benefits of breeding farmers; by supplying high-quality, safe and secure eggs and pork to the society and ensuring food safety, it will achieve the transformation and upgrading of the agricultural industry; the establishment of this project has increased the market share and brand influence in Russia. With its own advantages, Wellhope will provide the project with sound modern technical support for its overseas development to reap scale benefits and brand advantages. The ultimate goal is to develop the company into a modern enterprise with excellent production technical facilities, first-class product quality, advanced production and management concepts, and great influence in the field of feed production and livestock breeding in Russia.

Figure 16-3 The lab of feed mills

(Source of the Photos: the Chinese side of the Cooperation Program)

3. 2 Fields of Cooperation

By leveraging Wellhope's resource advantages on feed formula technology and efficient breeding technology in China, Russia Wellhope will facilitate the improvement in breeding benefits in the local market with a lower feed conversion ratio, a lower death elimination rate and a higher laying rate.

3. 3 Influence

By leveraging Wellhope's resource advantages on feed formula technology and efficient breeding technology in China, Russia Wellhope has shared the core knowledge and technology with its Russian partner and launched an efficient breeding model therewith outside China. This ongoing project can not only give full play to the Chinese entity's technological advantages in cooperation, but also fully tap the market advantages of the Russian partner. The cooperation can help the two parties achieve mutual benefits and win-win results, and jointly promote the development of technology and the market.

Case 17

Cultivation Technology Promotion for Fruit & Vegetable Greenhouse and Construction of Fruit &Vegetable Storage Warehouse in Russia

◇•

1. Overview

1. 1 Introduction

Shenyang Weiyun Fruit Co., Ltd. was established in 2013 with a registered capital of 5 million yuan. It is mainly engaged in fruit purchase, storage, sales and processing(packaging). Since its establishment, it has won the title of leading enterprise of industrialization in Liaoning Province for many years, and has won key project certification for 2 consecutive years in Shenyang.

The company has established a demonstration park for the cultivation

232

of high-quality cash crops in Krasnoyarkurtz, Russia, and set up a constant temperature refrigerated distribution center. In addition, it is currently carrying out a 15, 000-ton cold storage project in Novosibirsk with a total storage capacity of 15, 000 tons and an area of 15, 000 square meters.

1. 2　Significance

1. 2. 1　Help to meet the local market demand for agricultural products

The establishment of the local station of overseas warehouse service stations and the promotion of greenhouse technology can effectively reduce the response time of orders, improve theefficiency of logistics distribution, increase customer satisfaction, and ensure sufficient supply of agricultural products due to weather conditions.

1. 2. 2　Greatly reduce the cost of the enterprise

Logistics costs of agricultural products at home and abroad can be effectively reduced by using local constant temperature refrigerators for storage, thus offering the price a leading position in the local fruit and vegetable sales market.

2. Implementation

2. 1　Completed Projects

Shenyang Weiyun Fruit Co., Ltd. began to carry out a project to promote the planting technology of fruits and vegetables greenhouse in 2017. It has completed the preparation of agricultural materials such as seeds, chemical fertilizers, pesticides, and soil raking, sowing, fertilizer and pesticide application, field management work, and preliminary exchanges of agricultural technology with Russian scientific research institutions and local farmers.

At present, the company has set up a demonstration park for planting high-quality cash crops in Krasnoyarkutz, Russia, with an investment of 1.2 million yuan, leased 11.33 hectares of land, built 15 greenhouses for fruits and vegetables, and a refrigerated distribution center with constant temperature.

2.2　Ongoing Projects

At present, Shenyang WeiyunFruit Co., Ltd. is constructing a 15,000-ton cold storage construction project in Novosibirsk (See Figure 17-1).

The construction of warehousing and logistics will provide supporting services for overseas warehouses, and high-quality products warehousing, logistics and distribution services for domestic and foreign markets.

The completion of the project will effectively radiate to large supermarket chains such as local X5 supermarket chains (more than 1,800) and Mattemite (more than 5,000).

2.3　Future Plan

As for the promotion of fruit and vegetable greenhouse planting tech-

Figure 17-1   Cold Storage in Construction

(Source of the Photo:the Chinese side of the Cooperation Program)

nology, Shenyang Weiyun Fruit Co., Ltd. plans to expand the planting area of the park, expected to plant at least 11. 33 hectares of tomatoes, 8. 67 hectares of cucumbers, etc.

Shenyang Weiyun Fruit Co., Ltd. will continue to organize agro-technical extension, increase demonstration and promotion. Its goal is to promote high-quality fruit and vegetable crops in the local area of more than 33. 33 hectares, of which the planting of 20 hectares of tomatoes and 13. 33 hectares of cucumbers can increase the income by 780, 000 yuan and 500, 000 yuan respectively.

Regarding the construction of fruit and vegetable fresh-keeping warehouse, the company plans to complete the construction of existing projects, and gradually build large-scale warehousing logistics groups and storage supporting facilities, and invite more foreign fruit and vegetable operators, large chain dealers and other vendors to achieve long-term cooperation.

3. Major Characteristics

3. 1   Benefits of Cooperation

3. 1. 1   Creating More Jobs

The implementation of the two projects mentioned above have effectively promotes the development of local agriculture, solved the problem of local employment in particular.

3. 1. 2   Increasing Local Agricultural Output

The implementation of the fruit and vegetable storage warehouse project can meet the local market demand. Relying on the high-quality fruit and vegetable planting demonstration park, the high-quality fruits and vegetables that are most suitable for cultivation in the Krasnoyarkutsk region of Russia are selected, the local farmers in Russia are trained on the farming techniques, domestic high-quality planting techniques are promoted, and local farmers' cultivation skills are improved. Some of the harvest of fruits and vegetables will be used for local sales, and high-quality fruits and vegetables are expected to be shipped to other countries of the Russian Federation in order to ensure the safety of local fruits and vegetables, build overseas fruit and vegetable reserve bases, and achieve both economic and social benefits.

3.2   Fields of Cooperation

With the construction and improvement of the project, the fruit and vegetable fresh-keeping warehouse is just around the corner. After the completion of the project, it will not only improve the construction of the entire foreign market industrial chain of agricultural products, but also speed up the trade output between China and Russia, and realize the common prosperity of bilateral trade between China and Russia.

3.3   Influence

This project has two typical characteristics.

Firstly, this project leveraged the advantages of overseas resources and domestic capital and technology to effectively complement the advantages by establishing greenhouses for fruit and vegetable production abroad and promoting technology.

Secondly, the project is no longer limited to the traditional agricultural production, but fully draws on its own advantages in agricultural production technology and bases. Through the development of warehousing and logistics industry abroad, industrial chain will be continually expanded, and the development of modern agriculture will be realized.

Case 18

Russia Display Center for
Famous Products from Liaoning

◇•

1. Project Overview

1.1 Introduction

Established on August 31, 2015 in Liaoning Province, Shenyang Ezhong Trade Co., Ltd. is a Chinese enterprise specializing in trade with Russia and having qualifications on tourism development, economic information consulting and other sectors. Relying on the rich corporate resources in China and the strong appeal of Russia, the company has jointly invested with the relevant departments of the Moscow Municipal Government of Russia to build the Russia Display Center for Famous Products from Liaoning.

The center is located in the Moscow International Food City on

Vorozeth Street in Moscow, with a total investment of USD 1. 8 million and an overseas warehouse covering an area of 20, 000 square meters. The center focuses on product display, experience and sales, combines O2O e-commerce to create a one-stop service platform(See Figure 18-1)which is integrated warehousing, display, sales and logistics. At present, the company has established complete e-commerce operation and sales teams with a number of well-known Russian brand equipment suppliers and service providers.

a. Exhibition Room   b. Warehouse

Figure 18-1   Russia Display Center for Famous Products from Liaonmy

(Source of the Photos: the Chinese side of the Cooperation Program)

1. 2   Significance

It can strengthen the exchanges of superior products and excellent projects of the two countries, promote the economic and technological cooperation and cultural exchanges between enterprises in the two countries, and provide complete solutions for cross-border e-commerce operators. It has made important contributions to the "Going Global" strategy of China's domestic high-quality specialty products, especially those from Liaoning. It has also increased the popularity of export products and enhanced the international popularity and competitiveness of Chinese products.

2. Implementation

2.1 Completed and Ongoing Sub-Projects

Preparations for the project started in 2016, and the location is in the International Food City in the New District, Moscow. As the largest food city in Europe, the Moscow International Food City occupies an area of 35 hectares, and enjoys convenient transportation, complete product categories and large customer flows from all over Europe.

At present, the basic construction has been completed, and it is ready for the displaying and sales of products. The main products sold at the display center are those from Liaoning Province such as inonotus obliquus products, tomatoes, colorful pepper, carrot and various types of flowers.

2.2 Future Plan

The next step of this project plans to do the initial processing, constant temperature storage, frozen storage project of agricultural products, invest in the production process and equipment of dehydrated vegetables and produce chaga tea for sale in Russia and Europe. In the next five years, the project will further strengthen and improve the platform service system, personalize service experience, commit to realizing the functions of Sino-

Russia logistics distribution center and establishing a Sino-Russia-EU sales and logistics transfer center.

3. Major Characteristics

3. 1   Benefits of Cooperation

The two sides have set up a joint venture which has obtained relevant qualifications, known Russian laws and regulations, investment environment and market demand information, and created an effective connection platform for information at home and abroad, which laid a good foundation for further cooperation. The Display Center currently hires 8 local staff members. With the deepening of cooperation in the future, the project will promote local employment.

3. 2   Fields of Cooperation

Based on the overseas warehouse in Moscow, Russia, the project will further increase the product accessibility to users and enhance the product popularity by creating an international marketing network that radiates its influence to Europe and improving the after-sales and logistics service system.

3. 3   Influence

This project actively responds to China's call for the development of the BRI (" Belt and Road Initiative") economic strategy, implements the implementation of China's policies on foreign trade transformation, upgrading and optimization, innovates foreign trade development model, and fosters new advantages in international competition. It will play an important role in promoting the further trade cooperation between China and Russia.

Case 19

Construction of Agricultural
Production Base in Russia

◇•

1. Overview

1.1　Company Profile

Suifenhe Baoguo Economic and Trade Co., Ltd. (hereinafter referred to as Baoguo Company) was established in September 2000 with a registered capital of 20 million yuan. It is one of the top ten enterprises in Heilongjiang Province of China, which carries out agricultural cooperation with Russia.

In recent years, Baoguo Company has built two production bases in Russia. Overall operating structure: Two wholly-owned companies overseas plus one grain bonded processing plant in China. The two wholly-owned companies overseas are Illina Co., Ltd. and Green Field Co., Ltd. Illina is registered in the town of Pogranic, in the inner region of Poglanic, Primorskiy Kray, Russia; the registered address of Green Field Co., Ltd. is Kamen City, Primorsky Krai, Russia. The domestic grain processing plant is Suifenhe Baoda Agricultural and Animal Husbandry Products Processing Co., Ltd., whose registered place is Suifenhe Comprehensive Bonded Zone (See Figure 19-1).

**Figure 19-1 The dometic grain processing plant of
Baoguo Company in Suifenhe
Comprehensive Bonded Zone**

(Source of the Photo: the Chinese side of the Cooperation Program)

1. 2 Significance

This project makes full use of both domestic and overseas markets to continuously extend the external agricultural cooperation industrial chain and development space. After years of development, the project has formed cross-border agriculture, and gradually established a complete industrial layout, that integrates overseas planting, breeding, grain transportation, and bonded processing. It works as a link between the upstream and downstream of the industrial chain. On the one hand, it has promoted the development of agricultural industry in the Russian Far East, on the other hand, it has also effectively maintained domestic agricultural products supply.

2. Implementation

2.1   Completed Projects

At present, the construction of two large overseas agricultural production bases hasbeen completed.

Illina Co., Ltd. owns 8, 870 hectares of arable land in Pogranic, Primorskiy Kray, Russia; Green Field Co., Ltd. owns 5, 220 hectares of arable land in Kamen City, Primorskiy Kray, Russia.

These two overseas farms have more than 300 sets of large-scale agricultural machinery and equipment, and have set up raw grain drying production lines, granaries, mechanical repair depots, pig farms, chemical fertilizer depots, office buildings, staff dormitories, and other supporting facilities, and more than 6, 000 stored pigs(See Figure 19-2). By far, a total of 160 million yuan has been invested overseas.

In addition, in order to further extend the cross-border industrial chain, realize the benign interaction between domestic and foreign industries, and make full use of the preferential policies of bonded and tax-free zones in the bonded area, Suifenhe Baoguo Company established Baoda Agricultural and Animal Products Processing Co., Ltd. in Suifenhe Comprehensive Bonded Zone, focusing on overseas food planting and returning bonded processing business. The company mainly carries out bonded processing business of abroad-grown grain. More than 90 million yuan has been invested in the first phase of the project, and the corn slicing production line with an annual output of 100, 000 tons has been officially put into production. The construction of an expanded soybean processing plant with an annual output of 50, 000 tons and a mixed feed processing plant with an annual output of 120, 000 tons have also been basically completed and have entered the trial production stage. After being put into production, 200, 000 tons of soybeans and raw grain will be consumed each year.

Figufe 19-2 Piggery in Russia

(Source of the Photo:the Chinese side of the Cooperation Program)

2.2　Ongoing Projects

At present, the above two projects are being carried outas scheduled, and have achieved notable results. In 2017, the overseas park covered an area of 12, 000 hectares and harvested more than 50, 000 tons of raw grain; In 2018, the overseas park covered a total area of 14, 000 hectares, and harvested nearly 60, 000 tons of raw grain(See Figure 19-3).

Figure 19-3　Planting Base in Russia

(Source of the Photo:the Chinese side of the Cooperation Program)

2.3　Future Plan

The scale of production will be further expanded, and cross-border industrial chain will be extended. The project will take strides on the path of modern and ecological development. Within two to three years, the planting area in Russia will reach 25, 000(See Figure 19-4)hectares, the output of raw grain will exceed 150, 000 tons, and the second phase of the Suifenhe Free Trade Zone Processing Zone Project will be completed. An ecological and brand-oriented agricultural cooperative enterprisewill come into being, which integrates planting, breeding, warehousing, logistics, deep processing of grain and animal husbandry products, and high-end brand marketing strategy to Russia.

a. Corn   b. Soybean

Figure **19-4**   Crops planted in Russian base of Baoguo Company

3. Major Characteristics

3. 1   Benefits of Cooperation

In this project, Illina Co., Ltd. and Green Field Co., Ltd. in Russia have greatly solved the local employment problem and brought vitality to the development of local agriculture. The two companies have 147 employees in

Russia, including 63 Chinese and 84 Russians.

3. 2   Influence

This project is a typical model for enterprises to establish agricultural production bases abroad for agricultural industrialization through investment. By establishing enterprises and agricultural production bases with the help of local land resources, the agricultural production costs are effectively reduced; In addition through the establishment of grain production and processing enterprises in bonded areas, the further expansion of the industrial chain could be realized. This project made full use of the advantages at home and abroad, extended the agricultural industrial chain, and formed a complete agricultural industrial system layout that integrates planting, breeding, warehousing, logistics, grain deep processing, animal husbandry product deep processing, and high-end brand marketing strategy. Thus it accordingly brings common development of agricultural industry at home and abroad, and has important implications for other agricultural enterprises as well.

Case 20

Korea-Russia Agro-Business Dialogue

◇•

1. Overview

Objective：To build a forum for exchanges among South Korean and Russian agro-businesses; attract investment in the agricultural sector. Strengthening cooperation.

Period/Location：Once per annum(held in the Far East and Southwest and of Russia).

Host：Korea Rural Community Corporation. Organizers：The agricultural ministries of Korea and Russia.

Participants：Government officials from both countries, and entrepreneurs of agro-businesses(covering small farms, agricultural facilities, and horticulture and agricultural equipment).

Content：The introduction of agricultural policies and agro-businesses of both countries. Business meetings between agricultural enterprises.

Budget:100 million Korean won per annum.

2. Timeline

The 1st Korea-Russia Agro-Business Dialogue was held on April 2018, Vladivostok. 38 agro-businesses from both countries (26 from Korea, 12 from Russia) introduced agricultural policies of both countries, exchanged information, and held business meetings.

In June 2018, a joint statement issued during the Korea-Russia Summit decided that the two countries would hold regular agribusiness dialogue(the following is the statement). Both sides highly appreciated the bilateral cooperation in the agricultural sector and agreed to hold the business dialogue in agricultural sector regularly.

The Dialogue was included in the "Nine Bridge Strategic Plan" on February 2019. Establish an entrepreneur exchange forum to create a good environment for investment through dialogue such as business dialogue in agricultural sector.

The 2nd Korea-Russia Agro-Business Dialogue was held on June 2019, Moscow. 86 agro-businesses from both countries(23 from Korea, 63 from Russia) introduced their businesses, and had business meetings (co-hosted by the Korea Rural Community Corporation, and Korea Trade-Investment Promotion Agency). The agriculture ministries of both countries and the Presidential Committee on Northern Economic Cooperation participated in the event, and Korea delivered presentation on the New Northern Policy and cooperative policies in the agricultural sector.

3. Major Achievements

It has set up a platform to promote practical cooperation and exchanges between agro-businesses of the two countries. Provided meeting agenda for participating companies and assisted them to explore new markets.

Major Achievements of the 2nd Korea-Russia Agro-Business Dialogue was held on June 2019, Moscow. 2 contracts worth USD 246, 000 for the crop processing facilities were signed. 11 MOUs on the cooperation of the agricultural high-tech cooperation were signed, such as the smart farm and drone.

Case 21

Sino-Mongolia Expo

◇•◇

1. Cooperation Overview

1.1   General Situation

In 2014, China's president Xi Jinping paid a state visit to Mongolia and promoted bilateral relations to a "Comprehensive Strategic Partnership". Under this framework, the two sides decidedto jointly hold a China Mongolia Expo every two years. The third China Mongolia Expo was successfully held in Hohhot, Ulanchab and Tongliao, Inner Mongolia from September 6 to 10, 2019.

1.2   Value of Cooperation

The Expo was organized under the Belt and Road Initiative. It is an important channel to promote regional cooperation in Northeast Asia through the establishment of the Mongolia-Sino-Russia Economic Corridor.

2. Cooperative Implementation

2.1 Completion and Ongoing Projects

There are about 1, 200 guests and representatives from Mongolia participating in the Expo. A total of 450 Mongolian entities have the opportunity to sell their products and promote their business, which is of great significance for increasing bilateral trade between China and Mongolia and expanding mutually beneficial cooperation.

2.2 Next Step

The fourth China Mongolia Expo will be held in 2021.

责任编辑:李甜甜
封面设计:曹　妍
责任校对:周　荣

图书在版编目(CIP)数据

大图们区域农业合作示范案例/农业农村部对外经济合作中心 编著. —北京:
　人民出版社,2020.12
ISBN 978－7－01－022734－4

Ⅰ.①大… Ⅱ.①农… Ⅲ.①农业合作-国际合作-区域经济合作-案例-
　亚太地区 Ⅳ.①F333

中国版本图书馆 CIP 数据核字(2020)第 241535 号

大图们区域农业合作示范案例

DATUMEN QUYU NONGYE HEZUO SHIFAN ANLI

农业农村部对外经济合作中心　编著

人 民 出 版 社 出版发行

(100706　北京市东城区隆福寺街 99 号)

北京盛通印刷股份有限公司印刷　新华书店经销

2020 年 12 月第 1 版　2020 年 12 月北京第 1 次印刷
开本:710 毫米×1000 毫米 1/16　印张:17
字数:191 千字

ISBN 978－7－01－022734－4　定价:78.00 元

邮购地址 100706　北京市东城区隆福寺街 99 号
人民东方图书销售中心　电话 (010)65250042　65289539